SPLENDORS OF
ROME
AND
VATICAN

BY

TULLIO POLIDORI

T.P.E. EDITORE - ROMA

CONTENTS

Forward

This Guide to Rome seeks to offer the visitor a clear picture, and one that is as exhaustive as possible within the limits of space, of the places that are note-worthy according to a pattern of visits in keeping with the traditional routes organised by the major tourist agencies.

The short stretch of time that is usually available to the tourist is not enough to visit the countless churches and monuments listed in the majority of publications of this kind, and a detailed description, accompanied by a dry list of names and dates, in no way, would convey the fascination of the unique city of Rome. So in this guide an essential selection has been made, leaving out details and facts which might only serve to produce confusion, and thus giving the memory more freedom to fix on sharply-defined images of works and monuments that are really important and typical.

For this reason we have aimed at a straightforward and simple style, avoiding any kind of rhetoric, to show the spirit of a civilisation which the visitor will want to retain in his mind's eye so as to return to it over and over again in his imagination.

We have also sought to show the connections and relations between monuments, historical facts, and the persons who have been responsible for these. In this context the historical events, as well as the political and religious ones, play their role as an expression of humanity, linking the past to the present and, we hope, these will inspire the visitor with a spark of love for Rome and its history.

The Editor

Museum of the Palazzo dei Conservatori. The Capitoline Wolf: Etruscan sculpture of the 6th century. The twins were added in the 15th century by Pollaiuolo.

The Growth of Rome

According to Varro, Rome was founded on April 21st of the year 753 B.C., when Romulus and his shepherds settled on the Palatine Hill; eventually they expanded on to the Capitol, the Quirinal, the Viminal, the Esquiline, Caelian and Aventine hills on the south - Rome's seven hills, all standing on the left bank of the Tiber.

753-510 BC **The first period under the Kings**. Rome expanded into the Latium area, through wars with the Sabines, Fideneans, Veientes, Latins and Etruscans.

510-29 BC **Under the Republic.** Rome continued to develop and expand throughout the peninsula, with battles against other races already settled there. In the Mediterranean there was an epic struggle with Carthage which began in 264 BC, and ended in 146 when Carthage was razed to the ground. In addition to this the Romans conquered Spain, Illyria, Macedonia, Greece and Asia Minor, and lastly Gaul, at the hands of Julius Caesar, who,in fact, put an end to the Republic. He was assassinated by stabbing in 44 B.C.

29 BC-475 A.D. **The period of the Roman Empire**. This was marked by a first phase of splendor, lasting for about two hundred years, during which the authority of Rome was extended to Mauretania, Britain, Fresia and Dacia. However, from the third century a gradual period of decay began, and this culminated with the fall of the Roman Empire in the West.

Principal events of this third period:
(A.D.)

14 – Death of Augustus. The great peace-loving Emperor devoted much care and attention to Rome, so that he could justly boast of having found a city of bricks and left one of marble.

64 – The burning of Rome under Nero.

70 – The conquest of Jerusalem by Titus.

117 – Death of Trajan, under whom the Empire reached its greatest extent, and the city of Rome had about one and a half million inhabitants.

272 – Aurelian, worried by the threatened invasion of Italy by the Barbarians, began the construction of the defensive walls around Rome.

312 – Victory of Constantine over Maxentius.

313 – Promulgation of the *Edict of Milan*, by which Constantine granted the Christians freedom of worship, thus ending the age of persecutions.

331 – Transfer of the capital of the Empire to Byzantium (Constantinople) to make the defence of the eastern boundaries of the Empire stronger.

410 – First sack of Rome by the Visigoths under Alaric.

455 – Second sack of Rome by the Vandals under Genseric.

471 – Third sack of Rome by Ricimer at the head of

View of Rome from Monte Mario.

the armies of the Arian Germans.

476 – Deposition of the last Roman Emperor Romulus Augustulus, at the hands of Odoacer, a Danubian soldier of fortune, who was acclaimed head of the Barbarian armies by various tribes - the Eruli, Rugi and Scythians.

476-1400(approximate): **The Mediaeval Period**. The history of Rome is linked to the growing self-assertion of the Pope as spiritual head of the whole Church and as the *de facto* sovereign of the city.

Main Events:

493-553 – Domination of the Goths in Italy, during which the prestige of the Bishop of Rome grew constantly.

536-553 – War between the Goths and Byzantium. Rome, occupied first by one army and then by the other, eventually fell permanently into the hands of the Byzantines. During their dominance the Popes created the basis for their claims to temporal power.

568-774 – Dominance of Italy by the Lombards.

728 – Donation by the Lombard king Liutprand of the Castle of Sutri to the Blessed Apostles Peter and Paul. This was the actual beginning of the temporal power of the Popes.

756 – Pepin, King of the Franks, assigned to the Pope the lands taken by the Lombards from the Byzantines. Subsequently the Papal State was created, including the Duchy of Rome and other territories.

774 – Defeat of the Lombards by Charlemagne.

800 – Coronation of Charlemagne in Saint Peter's as Emperor of the Holy Roman Empire, which included almost the whole of Western Europe in its area.

1300 – Proclamation of the first Jubilee Year by Boniface VIII.

1308-1377 – Period of the «Babylonian Captivity» of the Popes in Avignon. As a result of this Rome fell into decay and lost much of its importance; its population sunk as low as 20,000 people.

The Renaissance. Occupies roughly the fifteenth, sixteenth and part of the seventeenth centuries. It is characterised by an intense activity on the part of the Popes who sought to adorn the city of Rome; they summoned famous artists like Bramante (1444-1514); Michelangelo (1475-1564); Raphael (1483-1520) to Rome, and in their works these artists expressed the zeal for perfection and grace which is the hallmark of the Renaissance.

Main events:

1447 – The list of Renaissance Popes begins with Nicholas V.

1506 – Pope Julius II laid the fist stone of the new Basilica of St. Peter's.

1626 – Pope Urban VIII consecrated the new church of St. Peter's, the greatest witness to the commitments given by the Popes of the sixteenth century - all aimed at the attainment of an ideal of refined beauty and classical decorum. During the whole of the 17th century Rome was constantly embellished by works of the baroque style - especially at the hands of Bernini (1598-1680).

The Risorgimento Period and the Modern Age.

1870 – End of the Temporal Power of the Popes and proclamation of Rome as the Capital of Italy.

1929-1943 – Rome, where the Fascist government was established, felt the impact of the Roman Imperialistic pretensions of the régime. Grandiose projects such as EUR grew up, and little by little the picturesque aspect of the city gave way to the rhetorical style of the lictors, aimed at giving prominence to massive and showy architectural structures making generous use of marble.

During the Second World War Rome was declared an Open City; thanks to this privilege, hundreds of thousands of refugees escaped there from all parts of Italy, and many of them stayed there even after the war ended. Today Rome's population is over three million.

Via della Conciliazione and St. Peter's Basilica.

A famous view of Rome in an inspiring night atmosphere; Castel Sant'Angelo, Ponte Sant'Angelo and, in the background, St. Peter's. ▶
Reconstruction of Hadrian's mausoleum by G. Gatteschi.

first tour:
Castel Sant'Angelo,
St. Peter's Basilica,
The Vatican Museums
The Sistine Chapel

Rome, that great witness to a past rich in history, that great collection of artistic masterpieces which together represent the most complete and unmatchable expression of man. The ruins, scattered around everywhere, speak to us of the happy times characterised by the cult of power and military glory, but mitigated by a refined artistic taste.

Of the precious architectures of the past, one of the most majestic and imposing is undoubtedly the "Mole Adriana" or "Hadrianeum", more commonly known as "**Castel Sant'Angelo**". The construction of the magnificent mausoleum intended by the Emperor Hadrian as a sepulchre for himself and his successors, was began in 124 A.D. and was completed one year after the death of Antoninus Pius in 139 A.D. The members of the imperial family from Hadrian to Caracalla, killed in 217, were buried in the Mausoleum. In 271 it was included in the Aurelian wall, and in 410 it was sacked by the Goths of Alaric. It was first used as a fortress during the siege of Vitigis, another king of the Goths. During the XV and XVI centuries it took on its present appearance; and as it was built as a refuge for the Popes, their apartments were decorated by several of the same artists who worked in the Vatican. In case of danger, the Popes could reach it directly from the Vatican, through a covered corridor called the *Passetto.*

The name of Castel Sant'Angelo is derived from the vision of Pope Gregory I who in 590 led a procession to petition God to stop a plague; while

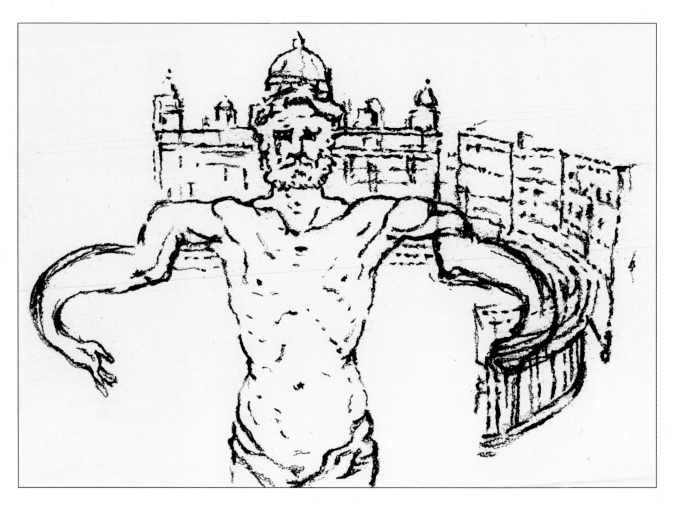

Mother Church opens wide her arms, to gather in the countless waves of pilgrims and visitors who come to her from every corner of the Earth. It was this symbolical embrace that inspired Gian Lorenzo Bernini's construction of St.Peter's Square, as evidenced by this famous drawing executed by the artist, in which St.Peter, arms outstretched, personifies the Basilica and the Colonnade.

St. Peter's Basilica and St. Peter's Square. Behind the Basilica, the Vatican Gardens; on the right, the Sistine Chapel and the ▶ Apostolic Palaces.

crossing the bridge he saw on top of the fortress the Archangel Michael sheathing a flaming sword, the divine signal that the pestilence was over. (Incidentally, the symptoms of the plague were attacks of sneezing and yawning. When people saw friends yawning and sneezing they made the sign of the cross and said «God bless you», as the Pope had ordered. This habit started on that occasion).

This place has also acquired a sinister fame as a state prison, you have its parallel in the Tower of London; many visitors will recall Castel Sant'Angelo from the opera La Tosca in which it appears in the third act as a prison.

Leading to St. Peter's Square is the **street of Conciliation**; this new, direct, monumental approach to the Vatican, from Rome, was called Conciliation to commemorate the signing of the Lateran Pact in 1929, and was inaugurated in 1950 on the occasion of the Jubilee Year.

The Vatican City

We are welcomed by the magnificent Piazza San Pietro, **St.Peter's Square**, the architectural masterpiece by Gian Lorenzo Bernini. 284 Tuscan columns arranged in a quadruple row and 89 pillars from the two huge semicircles enclosing it. The entablature is crowned by 140 statues of saints and the large coats of arms of Pope Alexander VII Chigi, who commissioned the work.

This Piazza was built in a short time (between 1655 and 1667) mainly because the architectural project was overseen by Bernini himself. The oldest monument in the square is the monolithic Egyptian obelisk, which stands in the center. Caligula had brought it to Rome to decorate his Circus and near it St.Peter was probably crucified with his head down.

In 1586 under Sixtus V the obelisk was re-erec-

ted on its present site and later upon it was placed the emblem of the Chigi Pope Alexander VII, the five small mounts and the star in bronze, this device containing a relic of the Cross. The two beautiful fountains were built at different times; the one on the right by Maderno, and the other by Bernini, in 1677, which was the last monument put within the colonnade.

Set into the paving, between the fountains and the obelisk, are two round stone slabs; standing on either of these and observing the colonnade, you have the impression that St. Peter's Square is encircled by a single row of columns instead of a quadruple one.

Visitors and Romans gather every Sunday on St. Peter's Square for the Pope's blessing and particularly on January 1st, Palm Sunday and, of course, on Easter Sunday and Christmas.

In the peace of early morning, the sun illuminates an incomparable scene: the immense Square of St.Peter's dominated by the Michaelangelo's Dome and encircled by Bernini's Colonnade.

The Swiss Guard, instituted by Pope Julius II in 1506, loyal through the centuries, is the Pontiff's bodyguard.

The Dome of St.Peter's or as it is affectionately called by Romans "er Cupolone" (the big Dome), an architectural masterpiece of Michaelangelo.

St. Peter's Basilica

Pope Sylvester I, in the year 326 A.D., inaugurated the basilica, built by Emperor Constantine over the grave of St. Peter. The Apostle was martyred in the Circus of Nero in 64 or 67 A.D., and this Circus had always been located where the church stands, until recent excavations proved that St. Peter's foundations were laid on virgin soil. This new fact has posed an archaeological question to which we do not as yet have the answer. The excavations also proved that the main altar of the church stands right over the grave of St. Peter. During the public audience of June 26th 1968, Pope Paul VI announced that the relics of St. Peter had been identified with consistent archaeological evidence. This was the result of the researches which started in 1939 under Pope Pius XII. The present church was started by Pope Julius II in 1506, and during the 120 years of reconstruction, almost all the major architects of Renaissance contributed in designing and redesigning it.

Bramante was the first, and he also started the ruthless destruction of the old church. The new one he planned in the form of a Greek cross, but both Julius II and Bramante died after a few years, and owing to the political and economic situation of the papacy, the gigantic undertaking didn't make much progress until the 71-year-old **Michelangelo**, in 1546, was named architect-in-chief by Pope Paul III.

Michelangelo's final project was altered by **Della Porta**, who completed the dome, and **Carlo Maderno**, who added the nave and the facade, and at Pope Paul V's command, changed the church into the form of a Latin cross. The new Basilica was consecrated on November 18th, 1626. Through the great central portal, under the **Loggia of Benediction**, from which the newly-elected Pope bestows his blessing, we enter the portico with the five bronze doors of the church. The central one was made for the old St. Peter's in 1445 by Filarete from Florence, (If you go to Florence you may compare this with Ghiberti's «Paradise Door» made at about the same time). At the extreme right is the **Holy Door** which is only opened every 25 years for the Jubilee Year.

When you are finally inside St. Peter's, you cannot at first sight appreciate its magnitude, for your sense of proportion is deceived by the scale of the various parts; you are more and more overwhelmed as you proceed and compare with life-size. A few figures are in any case eloquent; the length including the portico is 690 feet; the vault is 144 ft.; at the far end of the central nave, the dove of the Holy Spirit has a wingspan of five feet. The Church has a standing capacity of 60,000 people. Another idea of its size is given by the brass tablets on the floor of the central nave, with the comparative length of the greatest cathedrals in the world; second largest is St Paul's in London.

We begin our tour of the Church from the Chapel of the Pietà, where the finest sculpture of the whole church is kept. **The Pietà** (the Pity) by **Michelangelo**, which he made when he was only 24, represents the sorrow of the Madonna bolding Her dead Son and Her acceptance of the will of God. It is the masterpiece of Michelangelo's youth, still under the influence of Florentine sculpture, and it is the only statue he ever signed. His name is to be found on the sash across the Madonna's breast. The chapel of the Pietà was originally dedicated to the Crucifixion; on the empty cross we read the four letters (**INRI**), standing for Iesus Nazarenus Rex Iudeorum (Jesus of Nazareth, King of the Jews), the inscription put on the Cross to deride Christ. On the ceiling above the Pietà is the only fresco painting in the church, the Triumph of the Cross by Lanfranco, XVII century.

All that appears to be painting in St. Peter's, is in fact mosaic work, from the mosaic studio in the Vatican, which is the only place in the world where a painting can be reproduced in mosaic with perfect exactness. They use mainly composition stone.

Continuing along the right aisle and immediately on the right is the **Chapel of the Crucifix**, containing a XII century crucifix, ascribed to Cavallini. Opposite the chapel of the Crucifix is the memorial to Christina of Sweden by C. Fontana, one of the few women buried in St. Peter's. She abdicated and converted to Catholicism, which her father, Gustavus Adolphus, had fought against during the Thirty Years War and she came to Rome in 1655. Her grave is in the crypt underneath the church. In the next chapel is the mosaic reproduction of the Martyrdom of St. Sebastian by Domenichino, XVII century. In an open glass casket underneath the altar lies the body of Blessed Innocent XI, XVII century, his face and his hands are covered with silver. (The title of «Beatus», or «Blessed» is given prior to the declaration of Sainthood).

On the left of it is the fine bronze statue of Pope Pius XII by Messina, 1964. In the same aisle is the splendid **Chapel of the Blessed Sacrament;** above the altar is the gilded bronze pyx by Bernini, inspired by the Tempietto di Bramante in the Church of St. Peter's in Montorio. Behind the altar is the only oil-painting of the whole Church: the Trinity, by Pietro da Cortona. Beyond the chapel, on the right, is the monument to Pope Gregory XIII, by Rusconi, XVII century, the pope who reformed the old Roman Julian Calendar. There is a relief recalling this event which took place is 1582.

We return to the central nave and we find ourselves in the part of the Basilica built by Michelangelo. He planned the church in the form of a Greek Cross, the embodiment of the symbol of the Cross, while the immense dome suggests the idea of the sky being inseparable from the Cross. Almost fifty years after he had carved the Pietà for the old St. Peter's, Michaelangelo, most reluctantly, took in hand his greatest architectural work, which was to be the culmination of his extraordinary life. However, he didn't live to see his dome completed; at the time of his death he had raised it to the height of the drum. Although Della Porta and Maderno altered Michelangelo's original plan, we can still say that this is his greatest work as an architect.

Proceeding to the **High Altar**, on the right, against one of the four immense piers supporting the dome, is the noble statue in bronze of St. Peter enthroned. This is the work of the 13th century Florentine sculptor, Arnolfo di Cambio. (The feet of the statue have been kissed smooth by the faithful).

When you stand beneath the vastness of the dome, you see how everything else is dwarfed in sight, even the bronze **canopy by Bernini** which has the height of a five-storey building. We'll note, for instance, that St. Mark's pen, in one of the roundels of the pendentives, is five feet. Beneath the roundels with the mosaic pictures of the four

St.Peter's Basilica. Pope John Paul II crosses the threshold of the Holy Door of St. Peter's at the start of the Holy Year 2000.

St.Peter's Basilica. Detail of the bronze door by Filarete: the Crucifixion of St.Peter. The Apostle asked to be crucified head-down in order not to equal Christ.

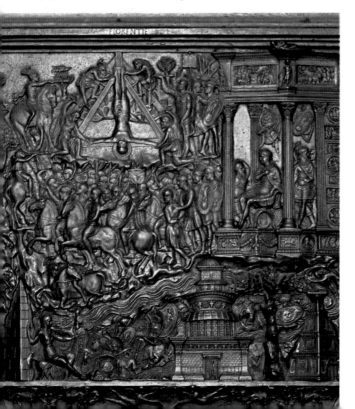

Evangelists are the balconies, decorated with the spiral columns from the canopy of the old St. Peter's, which gave Bernini the idea for his bronze canopy. At Easter time the principal relics kept in St.Peter's are exposed from these balconies. They are: the fragment of the Sacred Lance, with which St. Longinus pierced the side of Christ while He was hanging on the Cross, the statue of this Saint, by Bernini, is at the base of the pier; above the statue of St.Andrew the skull of the saint. The relics kept in the other two piers are: a fragment of the true Cross and the veil of St.Veronica, with the statues of St. Helena and St. Veronica.

Underneath the dome and Bernini's canopy, is the main altar, at which only the Pope has the privilege of celebrating Mass. In front of the altar is the lowered part known as **The Confession**.

Directly beneath the main altar, closed by a gilded grill, is the **Niche of the Pallia**, built in the sixth century, where the Pallium, a long strip-like vestment, was placed before being bestowed on the newly-appointed archbishops.

◄ St.Peter's Basilica. A view of the central nave with the Altar of Confession and Bernini's Canopy.

St.Peter's Basilica. The masterpiece of Michelangelo's youth, the Pietà. His name can be read on the sash across the Madonna's breast.

Beyond the canopy is the part of the church used for the most important ceremonies, such as canonizations, beatifications, coronations of the new popes etc. At the end of the absis are two masterpieces by Bernini: the bronze one is **Cattedra**, the Bishop's chair, held by four Church Fathers: St. Ambrose and St. Augustine in front representing the Latin Church, St. Athanasius and St. John Chrysostom, representing the Greek Church; above the Cattedra is the Glory of the Holy Spirit. The other, to the right of the Cattedra, is the monument to Pope Urban VIII.

The monument on the left of the Cattedra, of Paul III, is by Guglielmo della Porta. These are two of the finest papal monuments in the church. Encased in Bernini's bronze throne is a wooden chair with ivory ornamentation which according to tradition was the one used by St. Peter. A recent examination of the chair proved this to be the one donated to Pope John VII in 875, by the Carolingian King Charles II the Bald, when he was crowned in St. Peter's on Dec. 25th of that year. It dates from the ninth century.

Crossing the basilica, we traverse the left transept, noting on the right the monument of Alexander VII by Bernini, which he made when he was almost eighty years old, the last work of this indefatigable genius.

Then we come to the **Clementina Chapel** where there is the monument of Pius VII by the Danish sculptor Thorvaldsen, the only monument in the church by a non-Catholic artist.

Before entering the left aisle, immediately on the left, is a mosaic reproduction of the **Transfiguration by Raphael**, his last work which he left unfinished, and which his disciple Giulio Romano completed. The original is in the Pinacoteca, the Vatican picture gallery. Entering the left aisle on the right is the monument to the pope who only reigned 24 days, Leo XI Medici, by Algardi, XVII century. A reference to his very short reign are the roses on the plinth and the words *Sic Floruit*.

Continuing towards the exit, immediately on the right we find the rich **Choir Chapel**; above the altar is the lovely mosaic picture of the Immaculate Conception. After the chapel come next two monuments set into the wall, face to face: Innocent VIII, executed by Pollaiolo in the late XV century, and St. Pius X, whose remains are preserved under the altar of the next chapel.

Embedded into the following pillar, to the left, is the monument by Antonio Canova to James III Stuart, the old pretender and his children. The last chapel, the Baptistery, has a baptismal font formed by the cover of an ancient porphyry sarcophagus, probably from Emperor Hadrian's tomb.

St.Peter's Basilica. St.Peter's Tomb and the Niche of the Pallia.

St.Peter's Basilica. A spectacular view of Michelangelo's Cupola partially hidden by Bernini's baldacchino. The mosaics inside the dome were executed in the late 16th century after cartoons by Cavalier d'Arpino. ▶

◀ The XIII cent. statue of St. Peter attributed to Arnolfo di Cambio. The feet worn away by the kisses of the faithful.

Gian Lorenzo Bernini. The Triumph of the Cattedra and the Holy Spirit in Glory.

The Vatican Museums

Our visit this morning will bring us back to the Vatican City, again within the boundary line of the Papal State. Also this part stands over the area which the Etruscans called Vaticus or Mons Vaticus (Vatican hill), one of the places where the Vates, the seers or the prophets, revealed the omens or presages. The side from which we enter the Museums is surrounded by powerful ramparts called Leonine. They were built by Pope Leo IV in 852. In 846, forty-six years after Charlemagne's coronation in St. Peter's, the Saracens descended upon Rome and stripped the fabulous shrines of St. Peter's and St. Paul's, carrying off tons of silver and gold. The plundering lasted one week. After they had gone, Leo IV built a wall around the domain of St. Peter's.

The Vatican has been the principal seat of the Popes for about six hundred years. You will recall that the Popes moved to Avignon in 1308 and Gregory XI returned to Rome seventy years later and established his abode in the Vatican, which was another residence of the Bishop of Rome. It was not until the time of Pope Nicholas V that a plan was made for a greatly enlarged Vatican, to be the most ma-gnificent palace to house the princes of the Church and the myriad treasures accumulated through the centuries. Nicholas V was a great lover of learning and planned, at the same time, to rebuild the Church of St. Peter, which was later started by Julius II.

Guided tours can never afford more than two hours for this visit so we will confine our attention to the most outstanding masterpieces. We will start with the **Octagonal Courtyard** where we find the most famous statues.

The Octagonal or Belvedere Courtyard

The octagonal **Courtyard of Belvedere** was the center of the villa, built by Bramante for Pope Innocent VIII at the end of the fifteenth century. In one corner is the **Group of Laocoön**; it was found in the RUINS OF Nero's Golden House (*Domus Aurea*), near the Colosseum in the XV century. The sculpture represents the Trojan priest, punished by the gods, for the warning he gave his townsmen about the horse of Troy. The legend says that two serpents came from the sea and killed Laocoön and his two children. This is a remarkable work by Agesandros and his sons, Athenodoros and

The
**Octagonal
or Belvedere
Courtyard.**

Polidoros of Rhodes, from the first century B.C. Rhodes was, with Alexandria in Egypt and Ephesus in Turkey, one of the three great centers of art around the Mediterranean during the first century B.C. The art of this period is extremely realistic and the Laocoön group is most representative of it, with the desperate struggle of the priest, in the moment of agony, his muscles exaggeratedly tense, his sons, one already dying, the other turning his head hopelessly towards his father.

In another corner is the **Apollo Belvedere**, a statue believed to be a copy from a bronze masterpiece by the Greek sculptor Leochares of the IV century B.C. The figure of the god is tall, athletic and slender; he steps forward to see if the arrow he has just thrown has met its mark. Apollo was also the god defender and bringer of peace. This statue was found at Grottaferrata in the fifteenth century.

In the **Room of the Animals** are numerous works from different times, in which animals play a role. There is a copy of the Meleager by Skopas, and the group of Mithras, the Persian god sacrificing the bull to the Sun.

These first three rooms, built by Simonetti, were added by Popes Pius VI and Pius VII in the XVIII and XIX centuries.

In the **Hall of the Muses** are the statues of the nine Muses in the Hellenistic style of the III century B.C. from a villa at Tivoli. There are also portraits of personalities from the Greek world, Socrates, Sophocles, Plato, etc. all copied by the Romans from the original Greek works. There are not many Greek originals in the Vatican; one of the few is the so-called «**Torso Belvedere**». The statue of the Torso bears the signature of a Greek sculptor from Athens, Apollonios, son of Naestor; it is probably part of a fighting figure of Hercules. It was discovered in the ruins of the Baths of

Caracalla, and Michelangelo was most impressed by its powerful, perfect anatomy and refused to restore it, as he had been requested to do by the Pope.

The Round Hall contains a porphyry bowl in the center, from the ruins of Nero's *Golden House*. On the floor is a large mosaic work from Otricoli, a place 40 miles from Rome. Also to be found in this room is the head of Jupiter, fromOtricoli, attributed to Briaxis, IV century B.C. and numerous statues of Caesars and pagan gods, the colossal, gilded bronze statue representing Hercules; and there is Antinous, the favourite of Hadrian.

The Hall of the **Greek Cross** where there are two magnificent porphyry sarcophagy from the IV century A.D. originally the coffins of St.Helena, mother of Constantine, the one with the battle scenes; the other is of Constance, the Emperor's daughter. On the floor is a large mosaic from Roman times.

We are going to omit entirely the other sculpture galleries, and, returning the same way we came, we reach the **Sala della Biga**, (the room of the Chariot), so named from a chariot with two horses, a marble work probably of the II century A.D., reconstructed from ancient fragments. In the same room are copies of Greek statues, the **Discus Thrower** (Discobulus), by Myron, V century B.C. The original was in bronze and does not exist any more; the best copy we have in Rome is the Lancellotti copy, in the Thermae Museum. We cross the **Gallery of the Candelabra**, where you find some more interesting copies of Greek originals, mainly

The Apollo of Belvedere.

The Torso of Belvedere.

from the Hellenistic period, several urns and coffins from old Roman graves and the beautiful candelabra.

We pass into the **Gallery of the Tapestries** which houses a fine collection of original Gobelines, woven in Brussels in the XVI century. The cartoons were drawn by the disciples of Raphael and represent scenes from the life of Christ. On the opposite wall are the tapestries woven in Rome in the XVII century, depicting events from the life of Pope Urban VIII.

Gallery of Geographic Maps. The geographic maps, executed ca. 1580-83, are the work of Father Ignazio Danti of Perugia, a mathematician, cosmo-grapher, and architect. They represent the various regions of Italy with views and plans of the most important cities. The late XVI century ceiling is by G. Muziano and his pupils. Following is the **Gallery of St. Pius V**, with two large XV century Flemish tapestries, from which we enter the Sobieski Room, so called after the large painting by J. A. Mateiko (1883) depicting the liberation of Vienna from the Turks.

The **Room of the Immaculate Conception** was frescoed by Francesco Podesti (1858) representing the drafting and proclamation of the Dogma of the Immaculate Conception.

The Raphael Stanzas

The most precious paintings by Raphael are in the apartment built in the XV century for Pope Nicholos V, who was a real humanist, (namely one who in the Renaissance had devoted himself to the rediscovery of ancient philosophies and classic literature, which church men fought as pagan). Aeneas Silvius Piccolomini of Siena, later elected Pope Pius II, said about Nicholas V «what he does not know is outside the realm of human knowledge». Julius II decided to remodel the apartment and commissioned the work to several eminent painters. Bramante brought Raphael to Rome introducing him to the Pope. Raphael who was only about 25 years old, prevailed over the other artists. Pope Julius let him paint first the ceiling of the room called La **Stanza della Segnatura** (the Signature) where the Popes used to sign the Papal bulls and where the Ecclesiastical court of Justice used to hold its audiences. The young artist passed his test brilliantly and the Pope commissioned him to decorate the whole apartment.

The room of the Segnatura he painted in two years,

1509-11; the subjects the Pope suggested, symbolize the elements forming the human spirit, knowledge and virtue; the paintings on the ceiling are in close relation with those on the walls. The Roundel with the figure of Religion corresponds to the **Disputa del Sacramento** (the Disputation of the Sacrament). In the picture we recognize in Raphael the disciple of Perugino, the Umbrian master; the scene is symmetrically divided, the lower part represents Earth and famous theologians are on each side of the alter. The higher section represents Heaven.

The Trinity is centrally situated, starting from the top with God, Christ (sitting with the Virgin Mary, Saints and Prophets) down to the Holy Spirit. On the altar is the vessel containing the Holy Sacrament (the body of Christ), which is the focal point of the whole composition, linking Earth to Heaven according to the Christian faith. Some famous theologians are to be identified in the various figures: popes, Savonarola, Fra' Angelico and Dante Alighieri the poet. The perfect balance and symmetry on which the art of Raphael is based, appears more fluently conceived on the opposite wall, in the painting of **The School of Athens** which refers to the figure of Philosophy on the ceiling. The focal point of this com-

Raphael. The Stanza della Segnatura.

The ceiling of the Stanza della Segnatura painted by Raphael.

position is in the two central figures: the one in the red mantle, pointing to Heaven is Plato, who represents Idealism; the other in blue, Aristotle, pointing to Earth, represents Reality, the fundamental principles of philosophy. In the numerous group we recognize, in the olive-green robes Socrates; Heraclitus, the pessimist, in the foreground, with the features of Michelangelo. Raphael painted there several portraits; Plato is possibly Leonardo da Vinci. His self-portrait is in the group of the philosophers mathematicians, and scientists, on the right corner, where Archimedes, or perhaps Euclid with Bramante's features, draws on a blackboard. The self-portrait of Raphael is the face next to the last in the very corner, the beardless young man with a black beret.

Raphael has a fair right to be in that group for, as we see, his art is also made of mathematical precision and perfect equilibrium. The School of Athens is also the glory of man's knowledge and reason which permit him to create great works such as the gigantic temple in which this great assembly of the genius is held. The temple that is the prototype of the new St.Peter's Basilica designed by Bramante was left unfinished: through their impossing vaults the sky could be seen. It may be to remind one that Reason and human wisdom alone cannot bring to completion any important work without the help of

Faith. Above one of the windows in the lunette are the three virtues relating to the civil and canon law in the scenes below. Over the other window, the Parnassus with Apollo in the center seated on a rock, playing his lyre, with the most celebrated poets, Vergil, Homer, Dante etc. This room, more than any other place, is pervaded by the presence of Raphael and of the other great personalities he met there, and we feel the classic atmosphere of the intellectual world which permeated and exhilarated Raphael's alert and versatile genius. The young artist, after having painted for years little else than madonnas and saints, found, in the residence of the Head of the Christian Church, the opportunity of painting pagan subjects. It is a fact that the Vatican Palaces, the seat of Catholic Sovereignty, are also one of the greatest treasure-houses of pagan art.

Under the patronage of humanist popes, the Vatican became the greatest center of culture and art which ever existed in the world. We do not know of any other time in the history of mankind that so many geniuses met in one place. The visitor should bear this in mind when visiting the Vatican. The other face of the coin was the competition between these great men - a competition which was not always a fair one - being employed by the Pope meant glory and honour, but it also meant money

Raphael. The Disputation on the Holy Sacrament.

and security. The main contest occurred between the two greatest men, the two giants, Michelangelo and Raphael. When the latter started decorating the Stanze, Michelangelo had already been painting for a year in the Sistine Chapel.

The room of Heliodorus was partly painted by Raphael around 1412-14. On the ceiling are scenes from the Bible by B. Peruzzi, on the walls are depicted the subjects which the Pope had chosen to represent the triumph of the Catholic faith. On the back of the wall with the «School of Athens» there is **Leo I meeting Attila, the King of the Huns**.

The Pope has the features of Pope Leo X (Julius II did not live to see this room finished and he was succeeded by Leo X Medici). This picture is by the assistants of Raphael and we notice that the figures in it are almost out of proportion in comparison with the perfection of the School of Athens. On the opposite wall, by Raphael, is Heliodorus expelled from the Temple of Jerusalem, whe-

re he had stolen the treasure, by order of Seleucus Philopator. It is a clear allusion to the expulsion of the French from Italy. On the left Pope Julius II on his portable throne, wearing the beard he grew when he started the crusade against the French; he swore he would not remove it until he had cast them out of Italy. The interesting study of gleaming light in this picture presages the fine example of luminarism Raphael achieved in the **Liberation of St. Peter**, over one of the windows.

Over the opposite window is the **Miracle of Bolsena**. While a Bohemian priest, doubting the doctrine of Transubstantiation , was celebrating Mass at Bolsena, near Orvieto, the Host dripped blood. The miracle is connected with the celebration of Corpus Domini in June.

Pope Julius II is portrayed on the right of the altar confronting the priest of the miracle who shows dismay and uncertainty. Behind him anxiety appears on the faces of the people. On the priest's side wind blows on the candles, but the candles burn quietly on the Pope's side.

Raphael. The School of Athens.

There is certainty of faith, trust and calm.

In this picture we notice a remarkable study of color (the Venetian Sebastiano del Piombo was also in the Vatican then), with its predominant red tones.

So many other works were commissioned from Raphael, that he had to employ a whole school of assistants, whom he lodged in his princely house, never tiring of giving personal supervision to their studies, their works and their welfare. The **Room of Constantine**, entirely by the disciples of Raphael, was completed in 1525, five years after his death. Giulio Romano painted the battle of the Milvian Bridge and the Vision of Constantine, Francesco Penni the Baptism of Constantine and the Donations. The ceiling of this room was painted in 1585 by Laureti. **The loggias** overlooking the Courtyard of San Damaso were designed by Bramante at the end of the XV century, and all are decorated with frescoes by Raphael and his assistants in the style called Grotesque. This type of decoration was di-

scovered by the Renaissance artists in the remains of the old Roman Imperial palaces and the Domus Aurea, places which the Romans called grottoes. On the ceiling are scenes from the Bible.

Returning through the rooms we have seen, we'll stop in the **Stanza dell'Incendio di Borgo** (Fire in the Borgo) which is the last work in the Stanze by Raphael himself, but only in part. The scene represents the fire in the district near St. Peter's put out by miracle when Pope Leo IV bestowed his blessing. In this painting we notice another change in Raphael's style, who felt considerably the influence of Michelangelo's powerful personality. The strongly built figures, the study of anatomy and many details in some movements remind us of Michelangelo's art.

We leave the Stanze, where the Cardinals live during the **Conclave** (the election of the Pope), and we go to the Sistine Chapel.

Raphael. The Deliverance of
St.Peter; detail.

◄ Raphael. School of Athens,
detail: Plato and Aristotle, in
the Stanza della Segnatura.

Raphael. Self portrait of
Raphael and portrait of
Sodoma, detail from the
School of Athens.

The Sistine Chapel

The Sistine Chapel was built by Giovannino de' Dolci for Pope Sixtus IV, in 1473. Sixtus IV is the Pontiff who also built the Sistine Bridge (Ponte Sisto) over the Tiber, is the founder of the Sistine Choir, and one of the Popes who developed into greatness the Vatican Library.

The Chapel was named after him, and was intended for the most important ceremonies. It is in this Chapel that the Cardinals sit in Conclave to elect the new Pope. Its architecture is very simple, a great hall-shaped building (43 metres long, 13 metres wide and 26 metres high). A wonderful marble screen by Mino da Fiesole, XV century, divides the Chapel; one section, the larger one, is reserved for the clergy, the other for the congregation. The floor in the opus Alexandrinum echoes the mediaeval Cosmatesque art; the paintings engage our attention - on them more has been written perhaps than on any other work of art in the whole world. The decoration of the chapel reflects the Mediaeval conception, according to which the world was divided into three epochs: the first, before God gave the Laws to Moses; the second, after the Laws were given to Moses and the third, the period of grace starting with the Birth of Christ.

The two side walls were painted first. On one side are the panels with the **Life of Moses**, on the other the **Life of Christ**, The Old and The New Testament. These frescoes were executed by eminent Florentine and Umbrian painters. Starting from the Last Judgement, the scenes from the Life of Moses are as follows: *Moses and his wife in Egypt; the Circumcision of their Son,* by Pinturicchio and his pupils; *the Burning Bush, Moses killing the Egyptian and Driving the Medianites from the fountain, Jethro's daughters* by Botticelli; *Pharaoh drowned in the Red Sea,* painted by Domenico Rosselli or Ghirlandaio; *Moses on Mt. Sinai and the Golden Calf* by Cosimo Rosselli; *the Punishment of Korah, Dathan and Abiram* by Botticelli; *Moses giving the Rod to Joshua and the Death of Moses,* by Luca Signorelli and Bartolomeo della Gatta. The panels with the Life of Christ on the other wall represent: *the Baptism of Christ,* by Pinturicchio or Perugino; *the Temptation* by Botticelli; *the Calling of St. Peter and St. Andrew,* by Domenico del Ghirlandaio; *the Sermon on the Mount,* by Cosimo Rosselli and Piero di Cosimo; *the Consignment of the Keys,* by Perugino; *the Last Supper* by Cosimo Rosselli.

For two years these prominent artists worked side by side to paint the chapel; for two years each of them endeavoured to produce his masterpiece. The decoration was accomplished between 1480-82.

The Ceiling

It is because of Michelangelo's work that most visitors go to the Sistine Chapel. It is his work that rivets our attention to the exclusion of all others. Visiting St. Peter in Chains we shall see how Michelangelo had to interrupt the mausoleum of Julius II, and returned to Florence after a quarrel with the Pope. Later they were reconciled and he came back to Rome again in great favour by the Pope and hoping to complete the mausoleum. To his astonishment the Pope commissioned him to paint the fresco decoration if this ceiling, which at that time was painted only with gold stars against a blue background. Michelangelo did all he could to evade the commission, protesting that he knew nothing of fresco painting but the Pope persisted and he had to yield. It is said that Bramante, the fellow-townsman of Raphael and a bitter rival of Michelangelo, persuaded Pope Julius II to let Michelangelo paint the ceiling of the Chapel, in the belief that he would either refuse or fail as a painter. It was the competition which caused him to paint in the Sistine Chapel.

The Pope only wanted Michelangelo to paint the twelve Apostles in the lunettes and a decorative design on the ceiling; but Michelangelo proposed then to paint the whole ceiling and Julius II gave his assent. He started painting on May 10th 1508, and it took him four years to complete this titanic work, four years of indescribable fatigue and of stormy relations with the Pope. One day, tired of waiting for the work to be finished, at a rude reply from Michelangelo, Julius II struck him with his stick, after which the artist rushed home to prepare to leave for Florence, but the Pope sent his apologies and two hundred ducats, which Michelangelo accepted. On All Saints Day 1512 the paintings were uncovered, eliciting a universal chorus of praise. Three and a half months later Pope Julius II died. Michelangelo then went back to Florence. The scenes Michelangelo painted on the ceiling are framed by the painted cornices; he painted first an architectural structure, and divided the ceiling in its length into three bands; in the central one he depicted **Genesis**, from the *Separation of Light from Darkness* to the *Drunkness of Noah*: all around, above the side walls in the triangular spaces and in the lunettes, are the ancestors of Christ, David's line; alternately on the spandrels between them are prophets and sibyls. In the triangular spaces and in the lunettes, are the ancestors of Christ, David's line; alterna-

View of the interior of the Sistine Chapel.

Scene from the life of Moses: Moses killing the egiptian and driving the medianites from the fountain. Jethro's daughters. Botticelli. Detail

Scene from the life of Christ. By Perugino:the Consignment of the Keys.

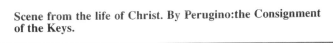

Pope Sixtus IV and his nephew, Cardinal Giuliano della Rovere, who later became Pope Julius II. Detail of the painting by Melozzo da Forli "Sixtus IV with Platina". Vatican Picture Gallery.

The marvellous self portrait of Michelangelo from the house of Buonarotti in Florence.

ENIA PONTES:
VAM.
MODA PORTVS:

On pages 34-35-36
Michelangelo. The ceiling of the Sistine Chapel.
Central section, from left to right: God separates the light from the darkness; Creation of the sun and the moon; Creation of Adam; Creation of Eve; Noah's sacrifice; the Flood; Drunkenness of Noah. Around the central section, the eight sails with Christ's ancestors. Inserted between the sails, the thrones with the giant alternating figures of Prophets and Sibyls.

tely on the spandrels between them are prophets and sibyls. In the triangular spaces in the corners of the Chapel are the four miraculous salvations of the Hebrews: *David and Goliath*, *Judith and Holophernes*, *the Crucifixion of Amman* and *the Brazen Serpent*.

Already at the first glimpse of this tremendous vision the visitor realizes that Michelangelo in this chapel achieved something more than human. He will also realize that the innumerable descriptions and the much picturing are not enough to prepare one for the impact which it makes, and, to be frank, we may at first feel a sense of disconcert. The time we spend in the Sistine Chapel is much too short, it will be difficult to immediately find the key to the understanding of Michelangelo's spirit and perhaps some people leave the Chapel wondering what really determines the importance

Michelangelo. The Creation of Adam.

of these paintings.

So let's try to see these works in perspective with their age and consider something which everyone can see: the striking contrast between the paintings of the side walls and the ones by Michelangelo. It is this difference of two totally different strains of thought, produced by the same epoch, which provides a ready access to the artistic history of the Chapel and the key to the understan-

ding of Michelangelo's spirit.

The paintings on the side walls hark back to the mediaeval concepts of life; they are still based on the mystical relationship which lays at the foundation of mediaeval life; they are still bound by the moral ideals involved in asceticism, scholasticism and the poverty of the Creature. Although at the end of XV century, the intellectual activity, the revival of art and culture, the rediscovery of

ancient philosophies, the scientific and geographical discoveries (the discovery of America), the invention of the press and so forth, had opened new ways for human development, (it was in the XV century that the world started moving faster), artists of the calibre of Botticelli and Perugino, when commissioned a painting by the Church were given a detailed description of the painting required; they would not dare to add anything of their own invention and they worked on a severe scheme (hard to recognise the Botticelli we know from Florence paintings: «The Birth of Venus» and «The Spring»). The result is that to the layman the side wall paintings look more or less alike. The figures depicted by Michelangelo were inspired by the dignity of man, by Plato's philosophy («the perfect man in the perfect state»), he broke through the bonds of mediaeval traditionalism, his hu-

Michelangelo. The Original Sin and the Expulsion from Paradise.

The Final Judgement

Michelangelo started the decoration of the l wall, twenty-two years after he had painted ceiling, summoned to Rome by Pope Paul III. **The Last Judgement** represents seven years of work. Michelangelo was in his sixties; during those years away from Rome his life had been deeply embittered and most of the works he had started he left unfinished. He had lost his father, whom he loved immensely; he had lost his favourite brother; he had lost his health and his faith in his fatherland. Rome had just experienced the most ferocious sacking of her history under Charles V, which people saw as a manifestation of the wrath of God; the Reformation of the Church and a movement for spiritual regeneration followed. The drama of this historical moment and of Michelangelo's life are reflected

◄ Michelangelo. The Prophet Isaiah.

The Delphic Sibyl by Michelangelo.

Michelangelo. The last Judgement. ▶

DELPHICA

man figures are perfect in their anatomy, strongly built and express intelligence; they are freed from their heavy mantles, as they are freed from mediaeval presuppositions and in them we finally see freedom of creation. (Michelangelo's two greatest loves were sculpture and freedom).

In his figures Michelangelo represented the precious gifts God gave Man, showing another dimension of the human race with the awareness of the possibilities and the abilities Man has to build his own world, to build his own future. Let us put it into modern language: Man who was to walk on the Moon.

ESAIAS

Michelangelo. Detail from "The Last Judgement".

in the turmoil of the almost three hundred figures which he painted in the Last Judgement. These figures were entirely naked and this aroused violent criticism. Michelangelo retorted by painting the Cardinal's portrait in Hell, with the ears of an ass and a serpent around his loins, to represent Minos. (The extreme bottom right hand corner). After the death of Pope Paul III, the figures were partly covered, Daniele da Volterra was the painter who executed the order and who was known ever after as «Il Braghettone» (the breeches maker).

The gigantic Christ, the inexorable judge, was criticised for being represented as a beardless young man. Around Christ and the Virgin Mary, are the martyrs, showing the symbols of their martyrdom; the face on the skin of St. Bartholomew, the Saint skinned alive (below Christ, to the right when you look at the picture), is the tragic mask of Michelangelo; the distorted face shows all his bitterness and alludes to all the wrongs done to him.

We find many more portraits in this picture, and a lot of details of interest. In the center are the angels blowing the trumpets to awaken the dead, represented at the bottom (in the left hand corner).

Other angels raise the elect to Heaven. We'll note the mighty angel raising, by means of a string of rosary beads, two colored men who deserved preservation because of their attention to work as well as faith. On the section to the right are the rebellious damned, pulled down to Hell. Beyond this screen of drama, we find the conception which had been the main concern of a Renaissance humanist «that a proper study of mankind, is Man»; in the end it is the human figure which dominates in these frescoes (you hardly see any landscape).

The paintings on the ceiling were the culmination of what had been done before in painting; and they are in painting what St. Peter's is in architecture: the crowning achievement of the revival of learning. The Last Judgement sealed the whole epoch. Michelangelo with these paintings said the last word about the Renaissance; symbolising all the newness, the freshness, the renovation and the innovations of this age.

The paintings of the Sistine Chapel, more than any other work suggest parallelisms, with current events of our age, and provide a link between Michelangelo's world and our own. In this, may be, we find the explanation for the great appeal that his art had to the men of all time.

Sistine Chapel; The Last Judgement; Self portrait of Michelangelo on the skin of St. Bartolomew

Michelangelo. Detail of the Last Judgement. On the far right, the portrait of Monsignor Biagio da Cesena depicted as Minos.

The Library and the Picture Gallery

Having reached the supreme work, as it were, of the whole Vatican Museum, it seems an anticlimax to try to describe anything else. On the way out we'll see the **Sancta Sanctorum**, containing most precious relics (from the Lateran) and in one room part of **the Treasury**, consisting mainly of presents to the Church from all parts of the world; note the fine ivories and enamels from Limoges. Contained in the **Christian Museum** are gold-painted glasses and bronze lamps from the Catacombs. Rather hurriedly we pass through **the Sistine Hall**, completed in 1588, by Sixtus V which is two hundred and twenty feet long; we'll note the contents, at least some of them, in the glass cases: the Vatican Codex B, the Gutemberg Bible,

the autographed letters of Raphael, Michelangelo, Martin Luther, Galileo and two love letters from Henry VIII to Anne Boleyn, thereby losing the title of Defender of the Faith, conferred to him by the Pope for his book on the Sacraments. It was Nicolas V who was the real founder of the Vatican Library; when he was elected, there were in the Vatican 340 books, when he died there were 1200. He employed hundreds of scholars and copyists.

We leave the Museum and you are recommended to make a return visit to see the Pinacoteca (the Picture Gallery of the Vatican), which has the advantage of not being large, but it contains Raphael's great picture of the Transfiguration and his Madonna di Foligno. Besides, you may be interested in visiting the Etruscan Museum, the Egyptian collection and the historically and artistically most interesting Borgia Apartment, decorated by Pinturicchio, where there are several portraits of the Borgia and Farnese families.

The Library: the Sistine Hall.

Raphael. The Transfiguration. ▶

second tour:
The Borghese Gallery
Piazza Navona
The Pantheon

Rome is the only European city which still has its ancient defensive walls almost intact: the Aurelian's Wall, named after the emperor Aurelian who had it built between 271 and 275 A.D., when the threat of Barbarian invasions started to appear impending. The walls encircled the city along a perimeter of almost 19 km. With three hundred towers and two thousand loop-holes for archers, they opened with fourteen gates onto roads leaving the city of Rome. Beyond a section of the wall and the ancient Porta Pinciana, extends Villa Borghese, which for a number of centuries was owned by the Borghese family.

At about a five minutes' walk from Porta Pinciana, partly hidden by the umbrella pines and the secular ilex trees, we discover the **Casino Borghese**, built as a summer house for Cardinal Scipione Borghese, the nephew of another prominent member of the family, Pope Paul V, and used mainly for receptions and parties.

The Borghese family lived in a palace in the centre of Rome where they still live. The villa, built in 1613, was designed by Flaminio Ponzio and the Dutch architect, Johan Van Santen who Italianized his name into Giovanni Vasanzio.

The villa was transformed into a museum in 1902, when it was sold to the State, along with the private art collection and the park.

On entering the museum we are immediately attracted by the ceiling frescoes of the entrance hall, the work of the XVIII century Sicilian artist Mariano Rossi, depicting events from Roman history and mythology.

The floor is decorated with five mosaics dating from the IV century A.D., found at Torrenova, on the Via Casilina; they show the combats between gladiators and wild animals. Along the walls are numerous statues of emperors and pagan gods. The museum has a large display of marble pieces and antiquities recovered from the ruins; it is with these, in fact, that the patrician families of Rome decorated their sumptuous houses for centuries. But the works of greatest interest in the museum are the statue of Pauline Borghese by Canova, the masterpieces from Bernini's youth, and the striking collection of paintings.

In Room I we find the statue of Pauline Bonaparte, the youngest sister of Napoleon who was

The lovely façade of the Borghese Gallery, XVII century. The lovely façade of the Borghese Gallery, XVII cent.

Antonio Canova. Pauline Borghese. Detail.

married to Prince Camillo Borghese. The sculpture was carved by Antonio Canova between 1805 and 1808 and shows Pauline as Venus Victrix, reclining on an Empire-style couch and holding the apple of Paris in one hand.

This world-famous masterpiece was commissioned by the princess from Antonio Canova, the most representative Neoclassic sculptor of the XIX century. The statue is one of the finest examples of this style which bloomed as a reaction to the mannered, pompous Baroque style which had preceded it. Neoclassicism was a new revival of Greek and Roman art, a faithful, but somewhat cold, imitation of the classic models. The statue of Pauline, on the other hand, shows a unique originality. In the lovely figure, all grace and charm, in the softness of the contours, in the wealth of details, you can see the artist's very personal zeal which thus dissembles the fact that he is following the canons of classic art.

In Room II we can admire the statue of **David** by **Gian Lorenzo Bernini** (1598-1680). Bernini, a sublime sculptor endowed with the versatility of the great Renaissance masters, as shown by his interest in architecture and painting; he had moved to Rome at the age of seven. In his long life there he served eight Popes and enriched the city with countless Baroque works. In 1623-24, at just 24 years of age, he sculpted the David on commission by his admirer and patron, Cardinal Scipione, depicting the biblical hero at the moment just before he throws the stone at the giant Goliath. The figure moves freely in space in a combination of exuberance, fury, and determination. David's extreme realism and movement preannounced the birth of the Baroque style (from the Spanish "barrueco", i.e. irregular in shape, especially said of pearls), of which Bernini is considered the father.

In Room III we find the group sculpture of **Apollo and Daphne**, which Bernini carved for Cardinal Scipione in 1625. The artist depicted the moment of the nymph's metamorphosis into a laurel tree when she was overtaken by Apollo. In this work the sculptor's talent and extraordinary technical skill can be seen, especially in the meticulous attention to detail and the plastic balance of the parts of the overall group. We can read the expression of horror

The Birth of Baroque Style

G.L.Bernini. Apollo and Daphne.

G.L.Bernini. The David.

The Hall of the Emperors and the Rape of Proserpina, by Bernini.
▶

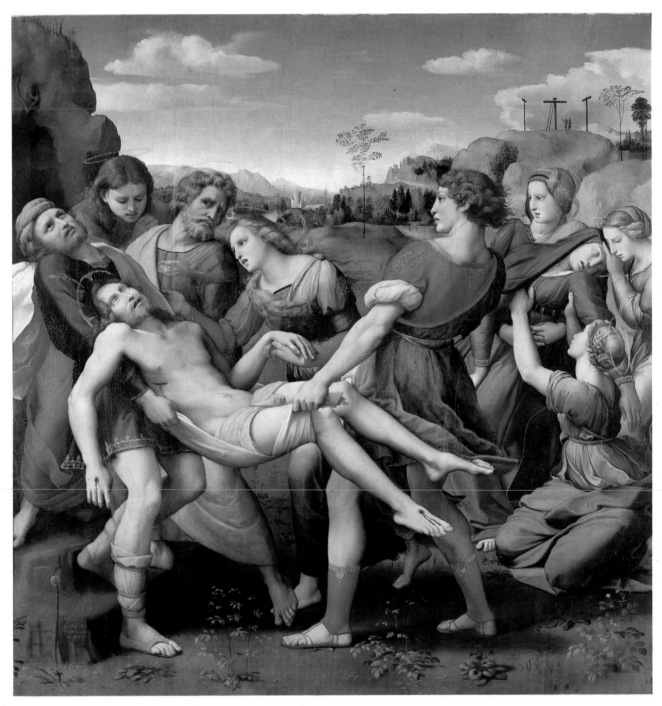

◀ **Caravaggio. The Madonna of the Palafrenieri.**
Raphael. The Deposition.

and astonishment on Apollo and Daphne's faces and, although there are some classical reminiscences, the work has all of Bernini's temperament.

In this room, the metamorphosis theme is taken up again in the painting of the mysterious sorceress **Melissa** or evil enchantress **Circe**, who turned men into swine. The painting, remarkable for the masterly combination of colours, is by Dosso Dossi, a XVI century artist from Ferrara.

Through a small room, which was once a private chapel, and which still contains XVII century frescoes, we pass into Room IV, or Sala degli Imperatori, a splendid room decorated all around with XVII century porphyry and alabaster busts of Roman emperors. The room is dominated by the **Pluto and Persephone** (or **Rape of Proserpine**) group in the centre, also by Bernini. This sculpture, which preceded the other two, shows in its technical virtuosity (the hand of Pluto softly sinking into the flesh of Persephone, her tears, etc.), the influence of

Mannerism, but the softness of Persephone's figure and the vigour of Pluto's movement show Bernini's exuberance and anticipate his inventions and freedom of creation.

The Baroque style remained in fashion for around two centuries, but fell into ostentation and became too pompous and theatrical due to the excesses of Bernini's followers. The reaction to it was the Neoclassic style of the XIX century.

In Room VIII, or Sala del Satiro Danzante, which takes its name from the sculpture in the centre of the room, a work dating from the II century A.D., perhaps a copy of the IV century B.C. original by Lysippus, there are six paintings by Caravaggio from the late XVI-early XVII century, characterised by the strong chiaroscuro contrast and the accentuated realism of saints and Madonnas. Because of this strong realism the Church refused several of his sacred representations, but Cardinal Scipione Borghese, a fine connoisseur of art and admirer of Caravaggio, purchased twelve of his paintings. Here we can admire the famous **Madonna of the Serpent**, painted for the Palafrenieri (the Papal Grooms), **David with the Head of Goliath** (the painter used his self-portrait for the tragic mask of Goliath), **St. Jerome Writing**, the **Boy With Basket of Fruit**, the **Ailing Young Bacchus** (another artist's self-portrait from when he caught malaria), and the **Young St. John**. Caravaggio, who died in 1610 at the age of 37, lived a short but adventurous life, and his art opened up new routes for European painting.

The "Pinacoteca" (Picture Gallery) is on the upper floor. In Room 9, opposite the top of the staircase, we can admire three paintings by Raphael:

– a **Deposition** dated 1507, commissioned from the painter by Atalanta Baglioni to commemorate her dead son. It is a plastically harmonious composition, but the extreme balance of the forms dilutes in the lyricism of the whole the motif of grief, which was the reason for the painting;

– a portrait of a **Lady with a Unicorn**; this canvas had later painted over to represent St. Catherine; restorations brought to light Raphael's authorship;

– **Portrait of a Man**; this picture, also, had been painted over by an anonymous painter and restoration revealed it to be attributable to Raphael.

Tizian. The Sacred Love and the Profane Love.

On the opposite wall is a **Madonna and Child** by Botticelli, a minor work, but noteworthy just the same for the intimate charm and accuracy of the drawing typical of Florentine art.

In the same room is another **Madonna and Child** by Perugino (Raphael's teacher), and next to it is a **Crucifixion** by Pinturicchio, the other major painter of the XV century Umbrian school. In the background of this painting we can admire a piece of Umbrian landscape, with St. Christopher fording the river carrying the Child on his shoulders in the foreground.

In Room 10 we can admire another gem of the Borghese Gallery: the **Danae** by Correggio, a great XVI century painter from Parma, compared by some critics to Titian for his handling of colour. The painting radiates a wonderful golden light from the gold cloud into which Jupiter has transformed himself to enter Danae's prison. We trace back over our steps to enter Room 14, or the "Galleria del Lanfranco". In the XVII century, Giovanni Lanfranco painted the ceiling frescoes depicting the council of the gods on Olympus, and strong caryatids all around which

seem to support the ceiling. This room also has other famous works by Bernini: a portrait bust of **Cardinal Scipione Borghese**, noteworthy for the faithfulness in rendering the physical resemblance and psychological intensity, and a copy of the same, sculpted in just 15 days, after the original had cracked because of a flaw in the marble. Other works we can admire by Bernini are the terracotta model of an equestrian monument to Louis XIV which was never executed, and the group of the **Young Jupiter with the She Goat Amalthea** carved by the artist when he was only seventeen.

On a wall of Room 19 is the large painting by Domenichino, **Diana the Huntress**, a typical XVII century Mannerist work.

In Room 20 we find perhaps the most famous work of the entire Gallery: Titian's **Sacred and Profane Love**, which everyone knows from reproductions; but no reproduction, however faithful to the original, can render justice to the silky softness of the brilliant draperies, the radiant fleshy tints, and the warm, clear light. Sacred and Profane Love is one of Titian's first works; the other three paintings

displayed in this room are from the last period of his life (the artist died at the age of 99). The **Scourging of Christ** expresses the dramatic substance of the event through the intensity of the colours. The language of colour is also used to express the interior meaning of the other two masterpieces, the **Temptation of St. Dominic** and **Venus Blindfolding Cupid**.

Coming out of the Gallery, we cross the gardens of Villa Borghese to reach the Pincio.

The Pincio

The Pincio Garden, as it now appears, was laid out by order of Napoleon Bonaparte, around the villa he built for his son, the King of Rome. In Roman times this area was owned by the Pinci family, and here were also the gardens of Lucullus.

From this terrace we enjoy one of the famous views of Rome, dominated by St. Peter's dome. Below the terrace lies the beautiful **Piazza del Popolo**, its center marked by the Egyptian obelisk which Augustus brought to Rome two thousand years ago, when it already was an antique, for it dates from the thirteenth century B.C. Down on the left are the twin Churches by Rainaldi, Santa Maria in Montesanto and Santa Maria dei Miracoli, while on the right is the much more interesting church of

Piazza Barberini. The Triton Fountain, by Bernini.

Santa Maria del Popolo, one of the museum churches of Rome. There are works by most eminent artists, such as Bramante, Bregno, Pinturicchio, Raphael, Sansovino, Caravaggio, etc. This is the church where Martin Luther celebrated his first Roman Mass. In the distance you discover several highlights of Rome; if you have extra time it would be worth coming to Monte Pincio to watch the sun setting behind St. Peter's.

On leaving the Pincio we'll pass by the **Villa Medici**, built by Annibale Lippi in 1554 for Cardinal Ricci and then bought by a Cardinal Ferdinando de' Medici in 1580; it was sold to Napoleon in 1803 and it houses the French Academy. In the Villa Medici Galileo was held by the Inquisition.

As we pass the church of **Trinità dei Monti**, founded by King Charles VIII of France, we can look down over the **Spanish Steps** and, continuing through Via Sistina, the street built by Sixtus V, which leads to Santa Maria Maggiore, we drive as far as **Piazza Barberini**, where there are two charming fountains by Bernini: the **Fountain of the Triton**, a sea monster blowing a conch and seated on an open sea shell, and the **Fountain of the Bees**, Fontana delle Api.

Piazza Barberini. Fountain of the Bees, by Bernini.

View of Rome from the Pincio terrace. In the foreground, Piazza del Popolo; in the background, the Vatican and St. Peter's Basilica.

The Spanish Steps

Through Via del Tritone and Via Due Macelli, we reach **Piazza di Spagna**, which for three centuries has been the tourist center of Rome. In its neighbourhood lodged Byron, Liszt, Goethe, Angelika Kauffman, Stendhal, Balzac, Hans Andersen and many others. The English poet Keats died in the house at the foot of the Spanish Steps on the right hand side. These steps should actually be named the French Steps, for the artistic staircase built in 1723, was the donation of a French diplomat, Etienne Gouffier. It was designed by the architects De Sanctis and Specchi, the latter being also responsible for the palace of the Spanish Embassy to the Holy See, from which the Piazza takes its name.

In front of the Spanish Embassy stands the Roman column supporting the statue of the Immaculate conception, this monument commemorates the promulgation of the Dogma of the Immaculate Conception, by Pope Pius IX in 1854. Piazza di Spagna is also the heart of the smartest shopping center and the artists' quarter; many of them live on Via Margutta and Via del Babuino, which leads to Piazza del Popolo. In these two streets you also find many antique shops and fine arts dealers. **The fountain of the Barcaccia**, the Old Barge, is the work of Bernini's father, XVI century. We enter Via dei Condotti, which is famous for its jewellers and most exclusive shops; almost immediately on the right is the Caffè Greco, which was the meeting place of Italian and foreign intellectuals and artists who visited Rome in

◀ The magnificent architectural setting of the Spanish Steps and azaleas exhibition in spring.

Nocturnal fascination at Trinità dei Monti. In the foreground, the "Barcaccia" fountain.

Statue of Caesar Augustus from the Via Labicana. Detail.

The ruins of the mausoleum of Augustus.

Piazza Augusto Imperatore

**The Ara Pacis of Augustus
(The Altar of Augustan Peace).**

Statue of Augustus from Prima Porta, now in the Vatican Museum.

the last century.

We take the busy Via del Corso and after two blocks we turn left to see the mausoleum Augustus Caesar built for himself and his family in 28 B.C., inspired by the Etruscan tumulus (sepulchral mound). The ruins of the enormous circular tomb are planted with cypresses, as it originally was.

On one side of the Mausoleum stands a simple modern structure containing a wonderful monument from Augustus's time, the **Ara Pacis Augustae**, (the Altar of Augustan Peace), which was erected to celebrate the peace Augustus established throughout the Empire and which the Romans enjoyed for many years after a very long war period.

Campo Marzio and Piazza Navona

We now enter the old historical section still called **Campo Marzio** (The Field of Mars - the god of war). This is the area where the legions were encamped during the Roman Republic; under the Caesars it was occupied by different public buildings, such as temples, stadiums, theaters etc. (Julius Caesar was stabbed to death in the Theater of Pompey which was where the church of St. Andrew now stands).

In this area is **Piazza Navona**, which is one of the most superb squares of Rome, built over the ruins of the Stadium of Domitian of which has kept the elliptical shape of the racing track.

It is decorated with three baroque fountains, the central one, the **Fountain of the Four Rivers**, is another product of Bernini's exuberant genius. The

Piazza Navona in its splendid
Baroque setting.

Night view of the Bernini
Fountain of Four Rivers.

four allegorical figures represent the Nile, the Ganges, the Danube and the River Plate. The monumental façade of **the church of S. Agnese in Agone** is the work of Bernini's rival, Borromini; a popular legend relates that Bernini's River Plate raises his hand so as to prevent the church from falling.

We pass the **Palazzo Madama**, a beautiful XVII century building, now the seat of the Senate, and the **Palazzo della Sapienza**, which was the Roman University until 1935, built by Giacomo della Porta and Borromini (the rival of Bernini) and finally we reach the Pantheon.

The Pantheon

The Pantheon

Sectional view of the Pantheon. Diagram of the proportions.

Interior of the Pantheon today ▶

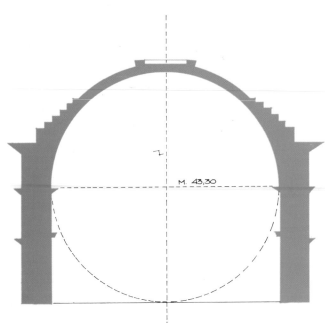

M. 43,30

The most important monument in the Campus Martius is the **Pantheon**, which is the only architectural relic from imperial Rome that has remained intact to us with doors and roof, surviving the wreckage of eighteen centuries. Pantheon is a Greek word meaning «all the gods» and the temple was dedicated to the main planetarian divinities and was built first by Agrippa between 27 and 25 B.C. The present temple is the one Emperor Hadrian rebuilt between 120 and 125 A.D. and probably designed by the Emperor himself. Its perfect state of preservation is due to the fact that it was consecrated as a church dedicated to St. Mary of All Martyrs in 608 by Pope Boniface IV who received it from the Byzantine Emperor Phocas.

The powerful structure is also one of the most harmonius buildings, unusual in its exterior with the pediment porch reminding one of a Greek temple and adjoining a classic Roman circular hall.

The great sense of harmony of the interior is due to its perfect proportions: the diameter is the same as the height, 140 ft., the dome takes exactly half of the height. If you imagine the dome continuing down in its curve, it would form a perfect sphere touching the floor. The Pantheon was achieved through a complicated system of relieving arches embedded in the mass of concrete from its foundations to the summit of the dome. The dome was cast as a unique block of cement on a framework with the coffered design on its reserve, using gradually lighter building material in successive layers to the summit, while diminishing its thickness from 5.90 metres at the base to 1.50 metres at the top. This dome, entirely built without reinforcement, has been the greatest in the world to this century (St, Peter's is three ft. less): an engineering feat of the first order which shows the profound knowledge of the techniques of construction required by the intricacy of calculation, which any layman can guess.

Buried in the Pantheon are some of Italy's great artists. There is first of all Raphael; he was also named architect-in-chief on the new St. Peter's at the Vatican by Pope Leo X and was given absolute authority over all monuments, buildings and ruins within a circuit of ten miles around Rome and devoted himself to the study of ancient buildings and ruins (it would not be inappropriate to call him one of the first archaeologists in the world). He certainly found in the Pantheon that majestic spirit of the classical world which inspired him and the other great men of the Italian Renaissance. Raphael died at the age of 37, on 6th April 1520, and when he felt the approach of death he expressed the wish to rest in the Pantheon. Over Raphael's grave is the work of his disciple Lorenzetto, the Madonna del Sasso, the Madonna of the Stone. After the unification of Italy, the Pantheon was chosen as a mausoleum for the kings; Vittorio Emanuele II and Umberto I with Queen Margherita di Savoia, his wife, are buried in the smaller apses to the right and left.

third tour:

Piazza della Repubblica, The Quirinal, Trevi Fountain, The Forum, The Colosseum, Saint Paul's Without the Walls

Piazza della Repubblica is better known as Piazza Esedra because of its shape, which retraces the architectural shape of the ancient exedra of the Baths of Diocletian. On the site of this monument there now stands the fine fountain of the Naiads, the work of the sculptor Rutelli, inaugurated in 1901.

On one side of this piazza stand the remains of the largest Bathing Establishment (*Thermae*) built during the Roman Empire - the Baths of Diocletian, which were completed in 305 A.D. In the sixteenth century, Michelangelo transformed the «tepidarium» (the hall with the basin where water was kept at a tepid temperature) into the Church of Santa Maria degli Angeli.

For many decades the rest of the ruins of the baths housed the Museo Nazionale Romano, one of the world's most important archaeological collections. Recently the most substantial part of the masterpieces was transferred to the building of the former "Collegio Massimo", not far away.

The Quirinal

After travelling down Via Venti Settembre and Via del Quirinale, we arrive at Piazza del Quirinale, and also from the Quirinal hill we can enjoy a fine panorama with the dome of St. Peter's in the background. The Quirinale is the highest of the seven hills of Rome, and in ancient times it was dedicated to the God Quirinus (the hill was occupied by the Sabines who came from the city of Curi). The palace of the Quirinale, built by the Popes in the second half of the sixteenth century, was their summer residence until 1870. It was the royal palace until 1947, and at present is the official residence of the President of the Republic.

At the centre of the piazza is the **Fountain of Castor and Pollux** with four old Roman statues of the twin gods with their horses, possibly Roman copies from Greek originals, found near the Baths of Constantine on the Quirinal hill. In 1787 was added the obelisk from the Mausoleum of Augustus, and in 1818 the basin in grey granite from the Forum where it once was in front of the Curia. Soon after the Quirinale we arrive at the Trevi Fountain.

Piazza della Repubblica. Detail of the Fountain of the Naiads.

Piazza della Repubblica. The Fountain of the Naiads

Palazzo Massimo, the new site of the Museo Nazionale Romano (Roman National Museum).
Palazzo "Massimo". The Discus Thrower. Roman copy of the famous bronze statue by Myron, V century B.C. One of the masterpieces preserved in this museum.

Piazza del Quirinale. On the left, the Palazzo del Quirinale; on the right, the Palazzo della Consulta, by Ferdinando (1732-1734). In the centre, the Fountain of Monte Cavallo or of the Dioscuri (Castor and Pollux).

Piazza del Quirinale; detail of the fountain of Castor and Pollux.

Trevi Fountain

The historian Pliny had included in the wonders of the ancient world, the acqueducts of Rome, known as Regina Aquarum, the Queen of Waters. In fact Rome had the most wonderful monumental fountains. During the Empire, when Rome had about one and a half million inhabitants, the city was supplied with water by fourteen large acqueducts. At the fall of the Empire, Rome was besieged and sacked, and to cut the water supply the acqueducts were all destroyed or seriously damaged, and all through the Middle Ages the Romans suffered from shortage of water. During the Renaissance the Popes restored some of the acqueducts, and it was mainly to celebrate the return of water that the famous monumental fountains were built; again Rome in the city of fountains. The most celebrated of them, at least the most renowned, from pictures, is the fountain of Trevi. The fountain we see now was completed in 1762 and was designed by Nicola Salvi.

It took thirty years to build and construction was not begun until two centuries after plans had been made for this big fountain. This very spectacular fountain is also the last important monumental work in Rome in the Baroque style. It represents the triumph of Oceanus riding through a triumphal arch on a seashell pulled by tritons and two sea horses, one tamed and one untamed, to symbolise calco and rough waters. The fowr woman's figures up above represent the seasons of the year. The water supplying this fountain is called the Virgin Water. On one of the bas-reliefs on the fountain, you read the legend of the Roman maiden showing the source of this spring to a group of thirsty Roman soldiers coming from battle. The first Trevi acqueduct was built under Augustus Caesar by Consul Agrippa, the same who built the first Pantheon. Tradition goes that before you leave Rome, you should cast a coin into this fountain to ensure you return. Trevi fountain is very pretty at night when it is floodlit, and it is also very centrally located, only two blocks from Via del Corso and one block from Via del Tritone. Continuing from the Trevi Fountain to Piazza Venezia, you cross **Via del Corso**, which is the main street of Rome. In all italian cities and towns there is a via del Corso, the central street where they used to hold, in the Middle Ages and the Renaissance, the Corse (horse races). On Via del Corso you still see several old patrician palaces, most of them made into banks or office buildings. Before you enter Piazza Venezia, the palace next to the last on your right, is the **Doria Palace**, still privately owned by that family, the palace being known as the most magnificent private palace in Europe. There is also a most interesting private art collection which can be visited on certain days. The

The Trevi Fountain

pearl of the collection is the famous portrait of the Pamphilij Pope, Innocent X, by Velasquez.

Piazza Venezia is the center of all national celebrations in Rome; its much criticised **memorial to Victor Emmanuel II** is dedicated to the independence of our Country. It was inaugurated in 1911, designed by Sacconi, built all in white marble from Botticino, near Brescia in northern Italy, and took 26 years to build.

In the center of the monument is the equestrian statue of Victor Emmanuel II, the king who ruled Italy after the unification, and underneath the statue is the tomb of the Unknown Soldier of the First World War. Facing the monument, on your right, is the historical Palazzo Venezia, the Palace of Venice, an early Renaissance building exactly 500 years old. Mussolini had his headquarters there, and from the little central balcony he made his famous speeches.

The palace is now a museum. The oldest monument in the square is on the left of the big memorial, the valuable Greek marble **column of Emperor Trajan**, erected in 110 A.D. to celebrate the victories of Trajan over the Dacians.

After taking pictures of Piazza Venezia and skirting the Palace of Venice, we go to the right of the Victor Emmanuel monument and we arrive in front of the two staircases leading to **the Capitol**. The steeply rising one, built over the ruins of an apartment house from the third century A.D., leads to St. Maria of Aracoeli, a mediaeval church; the other, gently sloping and surmounted by the statues of Castor and Pollux, leads to the Capitoline Square; it was designed by Michelangelo and called the **Cordonata**. On the right is Via del Teatro di Marcello.

If you continue along Via del Teatro di Marcello,

Piazza Venezia. Monument of Victor Emmanuel II.
The massive classical style monument dominates Rome's most important archaeological area, without succeeding in harmonising with it. To the left of the monument, along Via dei Fori Imperiali, are the ruins of the Markets of Trajan; to the right are The Aracoeli Church and the Capitol; behind is the Roman Forum and in the background the Colosseum.

you see, straight ahead of you the remains of **Marcellus' Theater** started by Julius Caesar and completed by Augustus (it had a seating capacity of 10,000 people) and to the right of it three columns of the **Temple of Apollo Sosiano**, built in the second century after Christ. Over the remains of Marcellus' theater the Orsini family built a palace, in the 16th century. You will also see two small, well-preserved temples built about two thousand years ago. They are the **temple of Fortuna Virilis**, the rectangular one built in Ionic style, and the circular one called the **Vesta temple.**

Beyond these two temples soars the lofty, XIII century, Romanesque belfry of **Santa Maria in Cosmedin**; the finest mediaeval belfry in Rome. We come immediately in sight of the **Tiber island** with the two old Roman bridges. The oldest one is the Fabricius bridge, built in 64 B.C. Horatius's bridge was also near here. Turning away from the island, on your left, stands the **Synagogue**, rebuilt in 1904 in the Jewish quarter, in the Assyrian-Babylonian style.

Piazza Venezia

Trajan's column

Piazza Venezia. Venezia Palace and the piazza on Republic Day, June 2.

On pages 74-75 A spectacular night view of the Monument to Victor Emmanuel II.

La Bocca della Verità
(The Mouth of the Truth)

◄ The Church of Santa Maria in Cosmedin.

◄ Piazza Bocca della Verità. The circular so.called Temple of Vesta and the Temple of Portunus, better known as the Temple of Fortuna Virilis, from the Republican era.

Santa Maria in Cosmedin: "The Bocca della Verità" or "Mouth of Truth". This is an ancient mask of a river god. The legend has it that the mouth would bite the hand of anyone not telling the truth.

Tiber Island seen from the south with the Cestian Bridge to the left and Fabricius Bridge to the right. In the foreground, the ruins of the Emilian Bridge or "Ponte Rotto" (the Brocken Bridge).

The Capitol

The Campidoglio. The staircase called "La Cordonata" , by Michaelangelo.

Reconstruction of the Temple of Jupiter, by G. Gatteschi.

Ascending the Cordonata you will note on the left the small statue of Cola di Rienzo, who styled himself the Tribune of the new Roman Republic, which he dreamed of re-establishing in the fourteenth century all over Italy. He died an ignominous death on the spot where in the XIX century statue stands. According to tradition, he inaugurated the 122 steps of the Aracoeli in 1348.

The Capitol originally had two crests; the higher one was the first citadel of the Romans, and later was occupied by the temple of Juno Moneta, which housed the Roman mint; from it originated the word money. In the fifth century, on its site, rise the **Church of the Aracoeli**; here Augustus consulted the Tiburtina Sibyl, had a vision of the Madonna

Piazza del Campidoglio. In the centre, on the splendid pedestal by Michelangelo, stands the copy of the famous equestrian statue of Marcus Aurelius; the original, recently restored, is preserved in the Capitoline Museum.

and was foretold of the coming of Christ, so he built the Aracoeli (altar of the Heavens).

On the other crest the temple of Jupiter was built in 510 B.C. It was the most important of the pagan sanctuaries, and with the 24 or 25 more temples built around it, the Capitol became the center of the Roman religious life, and the culminating point for triumphs. Between the crests was a hallowed spot (more or less the site occupied by the present square) so that, facing the Town Hall, the central building in the square, the temple of Jupiter was on the right.

In the Middle Ages the **Senator's Palace (Town Hall)** was built as the meeting place for senators, elected after an uprising against the government of the po-

pes in 1143; but the Senate was not recognized, and from 1358 only one Senator was appointed by the Pope, which explains the singular Senator. This institution lasted until the unification of Italy. Now the palace is the office of the Mayor of Rome. In medieval times this square was also used as a market place and as a place for executions. The Renaissance facade of the Senator's Palace is the work of Girolamo Rainaldi and Giacomo della Porta, XVI century.

The square, as we see it now, was planned by Michelangelo in 1538 for the arrival in Rome of Emperor Charles V, who, for his victories over the infidels, was granted a triumphal procession across the Forum and the Capitol, in the style of the old Roman

◀ **Bronze male bust of the third century B.C., known as the portrait of "Junius Brutus".**

◀ **The Palace of the Conservatori. Spinario Room.**

"The Boy with the thorn". Beautiful sculpture in bronze- Ist century B.C., hellenistic influence.

Emperors, but it was not finished until a century later. When Charles V arrived they had advanced as far as erecting the riding **statue of Marcus Aurelius**, the most famous equestrian monument of the ancient world. It originally stood near the Lateran and was believed to represent Constantine and that explains how it escaped from the turmoil of religious vandalism. The buildings on each side of the square, house the first public collection of classic sculpture in the world. **The palazzo dei Conservatori**, on the right, has among the other famous masterpieces, the bronze **She-Wolf**, and the **Boy**

with the Thorn. In the courtyard are the remains of a colossal statue of Constantine and a mutilated inscription with the word **BRIT**, the first four letters of the word Britannia; it is a fragment of the arch of Claudius, erected to celebrate his conquest of Britain. He was the first Roman Emperor to tread English soil, and this is the oldest reference to Britain existing in Rome. **The Capitoline Museum**, on the left, has the most complete collection of portraits of Roman Emperors and the famous **dying Gaul**. Beyond the Senator's Palace is the best vantage point from which to look at the Forum.

Capitoline Museum. The Dying Gaul. School of Pergamo, Ist century B.C.

Conservatory Museum. The Esquiline Venus. Ist century B.C.

Piazza del Campidoglio (Capitol Square) seen from above. One of the perspectives of this Piazza as planned by Michaelangelo. ▶

Capitoline Museum. Portrait of a woman, Ist century B.C.

The Roman Forum

From there you discover that the City Hall rose over mediaeval buildings (still visible are the towers at the corners) which in turn had been built upon the **Tabularium**, the Records Office, where the Tabulae (the Tablets) were kept. It was built by Sulla in 78 B.C. This is also the precipitous face of the Capitol, commonly known as the **Rock of Tarpeia**, the girl who betrayed the Citadel to the Sabines and was killed by them. The traitors of Rome were executed by being hurled from the summit of the Rock.

At the foot of the Capitol, where the Clivus Capitolinus begins, (the rising Roman street with

◄ The Roman Forum and the Colosseum in an evocative night picture. p.85

Roman Forum. View from south, towards the Capitol. At the right the Arch of Septimius Severus and at the left the remains of the Temple of Saturn. In the center the Column of Phocas and the three columns of the Temple of Vespasian. In the background the Palazzo Senatorio which rests on the ruins of the Tabularium.

The so-called Tomb of Romulus.

The Forum as it is today.

Reconstruction of the Roman Forum. In the foreground from left to right: the Arch of Septimius Severus, the Rostra, the Column of Phocas, and the Temple of Saturn. In the middle ground: behind the Arch of Septimius Severus, the Curia and the Basilica Emilia; to the right, the Basilica Julia. Further behind, from the left: the Temple of Antoninus and Faustina, the Temple of Julius Caesar, the small circular Temple of Vesta, and the Temple of the Dioscuri (Castor and Pollux). In the background to the left: the Colosseum behind the Basilica of Maxentius and the Temple of Venus and Rome; in the centre behind the Temple of Vesta, the House of the Vestals; to the right, on the Palatine Hill, the Imperial Palaces.

the original paving still on the site) we notice the remains of three temples. They are: the **Porticus Deorum Consentium**, or the temple of the Twelve Gods, restored as we read in the inscription in 368, A.D., the last reaction of paganism. Right under the slope of the Capitol are the three Corinthian columns of the **Temple of Vespasian**, started by Titus and finished by Domitian in 89 A.D.; next to it are a platform and a few marble blocks, all that is left of the **Temple of Concord**, dedicated in 367 B.C. to commemorate the victory of the plebeians, when the Licinio-Sextian laws were passed, and plebeians were permitted to be elected consuls. That was one of the political victories, which gave the letters S.P.Q.R. their meaning. **S.P.Q.R.** stands for **Senatus Populus Que Romanus**, the Senate and the People of Rome.

Across the modern road which separates the Capitol from the Forum are the eight columns of the **Temple of Saturn**, where the state treasure was kept; the temple was built in 497 B.C.; the ionic columns of the portico belong to the reconstruction of the IV century A.D. Near the temple of Saturn, under a protective roof, is the Vulcanal, or **Altar of Vulcano**, sacred to the forge, which according to tradition, was founded by Romulus, who made a pact near it with the Sabine King, Titus Tatius, after the rape of the Sabine women. The other place, which dates from the time of Romulus, which we can still see is the **Comitium**, the small open space between the Curia and the arch of Septimius Severus, where also the **Rostra** was, the platform from which orators used to address the people assembled in the Comitium. In this place we also find the **Lapis Niger**, a black marble stone inserted into the pavement, marking a sacred spot. Beneath

View of the area of the "comitium" in an 18th-century engraving by Piranesi. We can recognize the Column of Phocas, the half-buried Arch of Septimius Severus, and the Santi Luca e Martina Church, rebuilt in 17th century.

From the same period is this beautiful panoramic view of the Roman Forum seen from the Capitol, in an engraving ▶ by G. Vasi.

Arco di Settimio Severo.

ROMA QVANTA FVIT · IPSA RVINA DOCET

Le Rovine delle antiche magnificenze di Roma che si veggono nel Campo Vaccino.

Da Giuseppe Vasi disegnato e inciso l'anno 1772.

the Lapis Niger are kept remains of monuments, among the earliest in the Forum, the so-called **Tomb of Romulus**, and a truncated cone-shaped column with an inscription in archaic Latin letters, which resemble the Greek alphabet.

The superb triumphal **Arch of Septimius Severus** was dedicated in 203 by Caracalla and Geta, his sons, and, after Caracalla killed Geta, he erased his brother's name from the inscription. The present one dates from 305 A.D., and was rebuilt under Diocletian.

The Roman Senate, the Council of the Elders (from Latin "senex" - old), was the most permanent element in the Roman constitution; it may have been started by Romulus who chose 100 of his best subjects. At first only patricians were eligible, but later plebeians were also admitted. Under the Republic it was the chief governing body (510 B.C. to 29 B.C.); under the Empire (29 B.C. to 475 A.D.) it lost its independence of action. The senators, who met in the present Curia, were little more than ciphers. Built over the secretariat of the Senate, on the left of the Curia, is the Baroque **Church of SS. Luca and Martina**. In the open space on the right are the remains of the **Basilica**

Aemilia, built in 79 B.C. The basilica is a type of building with a distinctive architecture which played an important role in the life of the Romans; these great public halls, of Greek inspiration, served mainly for general meetings and business transactions, but were also used as law courts, like the **Basilica Julia**, on side of the Forum, rebuilt by Julius Caesar over the old Sempronia. Near the ruins of the Julian Basilica stands a single column, the last monument added to the Forum and dedicated in 608 A.D. to the Byzantine usurper **Phocas**, who donated the Pantheon to Pope Boniface IV.

Further down, silhouetted against the dark mass of the Palatine, at the far end on the right, soar the three magnificent columns of the **Temple of Castor and Pollux**, the brothers of Helen of Troy, which is one of the oldest temples; it was dedicated in 484 B.C. According to the legend, the twin gods brought to Rome the news of the victory of Lake Regillus, the final victory over the deposed Tarquin dynasty. To the left of the temple of Castor and Pollux, are the ruins of the small circular white **temple of Vesta**, whose cult survived immutable for about a thousand years. In that small temple the sacred fire burnt, symbol of the perpetuity of the

◀ **The Arch of Titus and the Sacred Way.**   Arch of Titus. The triumph over the Jews and the spoils from the Temple.

Roman State and of the household fire.

These ruins consist of fragments of the last reconstruction of the Vesta temple, in 191 A.D. Behind the temple are the remains of the house of the Vestal Virgins, who kept the fire alive; they were maintained by the State, enjoyed great influence, and after thirty years of austerity, they could leave the order and get married, but if they transgressed the oath of virginity, were entombed alive. On the left of the Vesta Temple are the scanty remains of the **Altar of Caesar**, the altar of the temple built over the spot where the body of Caesar was cremated on the improvised pyre, near the old Rostra, from which Mark Antony delivered his famous oration. At the far end of the Forum on the left, are the high steps and the Corinthian columns of the pronaos of the Temple of Antoninus and Faustina, the parents of Marcus Aurelius; the temple was dedicated in 141 A.D. and was made into a Christian Church, dedicated to **San Lorenzo in Miranda**; beyond the columns of the portico is the modest facade of 1602.

Beyond this temple stands another mediaeval Church, Santa Maria Novella, which rose over the ruins of **the temple of Venus and Rome**, built by Hadrian, and the vast mass of the **Basilica of Constantine or Maxentius** which towers behind it. In the far background stands the **Arch of Titus**, erected in A.D. 81, eleven years after the conquest of Jerusalem, which has a relief representing the spoils of the Temple.

After identifying the most outstanding landmarks of the Roman Forum let us try and picture something of its early days and comprehend the part which this square played in the history of Rome and in the evolution of mankind. The Forum, as we see, is in a depression of the terrain lying between the Palatine, the Quirinal and the Capitol. The Sabines lived on the Quirinale, Rome was founded by Romulus on the Palatine in 753 B.C. and this valley made from the very beginning a natural meeting point for those primitive people. This supplies the explanation for the center of Rome's development here. The Forum was always revered by the Romans as the cradle of their institutions, as here they established the first elements of an organised society, such as counting, measuring, monetary system, political and religious organization etc. In the oldest inscriptions the first numbers we find are five and ten, the number of fingers, for measurements they used the length of the foot.

The inhabitants of the pastoral villages on the seven hills counted their wealth in heads of cattle, and that was their first currency. The official rate of exchange, for a long time, was ten sheep to one cow (in Latin sheep is "pecus", from it originated the word pecuniary). The second Roman King, Numa Pompilius, coordinated the State Religion and founded the Vesta Temple; under the kings the buildings in the Forum were mainly of social and religious nature. Under the Republic our Forum became splendid and was the real center of city life, with its basilicas and temples, surrounded by tall buildings and colonnades, lined with attractive shops, and was also the scene of triumphs and sacrifices. With the death of Caesar (44 B.C.) and the accession of Augustus (29 B.C.) the Republic perished and that was the end of the free constitution and the beginning of the decline of the old Forum. With the spoils of the Gallic war Julius Caesar built his new Forum, at the same time as he built the Saepta Julia, great halls for political meetings. Augustus, Nerva, Vespasian and Trajan are the emperors who continued the reconstruction of the center of Rome on a larger scale, (under Trajan Rome had a population of one and a half million inhabitants). The Palatine, which during the Republic had been a fine residential quarter, was occupied by the imperial palaces; it became the new center of the Roman world. After the great days of the Republic, the power of the emperors replaced the power of the Senate, the letters **SPQR** lost their meaning and the voice of the people was never heard 'again. The old Forum became a place of idle gossip. The tremendous riches extorted from the conquered provinces caused profound psychological changes in the Romans. The most important changes were the decay of their morals and the loss of their stoic virtues of discipline, industry and frugality. The army was formed mainly from barbarian mercenaries, who were led by romanized barbarian commanders. To this add the greed of the soldiers (Claudius raised to the throne by the soldiers in 41 A.D. was the first to give them a salary bonus, which was subsequently exacted as a legal claim on the accession of every new emperor. More than once the Empire was sold to the best bidder by public auction). These are some of the reasons for the decline and fall of the Roman Empire. The mother city of Western Civilisation fell in 475 A.D., was invaded and sacked twice before then, in 410 by the Goths of Alaric and in 455 by the Vandals of Genseric. It is, in any case, in the ruins of the old Forum, that we see the starting point of the power of Rome, of what we are pleased to call Civilisation, by which we mean the Western World, because Rome is not just the capital of the ancient world, not just the capital of united Italy, not just the capital of Christianity, but Rome is Ours.

From the Forum we proceed to the Colosseum and near the Arch of Septimius Severus on the left is **the Mamertine prison**, the old Roman state prison

Roman Forum. The remains of the Basilica of Maxentius and below, a reconstruction of the same from a drawing by G.Gatteschi.

Museum of Roman Civilization. The model of Imperial Rome- reconstruction by the architect I.Gismondi. Detail of the monumenta area.

The Colosseum and the Circus Maximus and, between them, the area of the Fora and the Palatine can easily be distinguished.

The Avenue of the Imperial Fora

where St. Peter and St. Paul were kept prisoners, and where one of St. Peter's chains was found and where St. Paul wrote his last epistles. Over the prison now stands the small church of St. Joseph and close by are the remains of **Julius Caesar's Forum**, the part of the new city center which he started building. Across the **avenue of the Imperial Fora** are the ruins of the section built by Nerva and by Augustus (there are three columns left of the **Mars Temple**) and the ruins of the enormous market place built by Trajan in 110 A.D.

When you have the imposing structure of the Colosseum in front of you, on your right you see the remains of the **Basilica** started by **Maxentius**, and completed by Constantine in the fourth century A.D. On a wall are four marble maps which illustrate the growth of the Roman Empire, from the beginning, in the 8th century B.C. to Emperor Trajan's death in 117 A.D., when the Empire reached its largest extension. Approaching the Colosseum, on the right, you admire the majestic beauty of the **Arch of Constantine**, inaugurated in 315 A.D. It celebrates the final victory of Emperor Constantine and it marks the beginning of Rome as a Christian State.

On the left of the Colosseum is the area, partly occupied by public gardens, laid out over the ruins of **Nero's Domus Aurea**. This part of Rome, before the famous fire, was densely populated and was a large,

Via dei Fori Imperiali. The statue of Julius Caesar.

The ruins of the Forum of Julius Caesar with the three columns of the Temple of Venus.

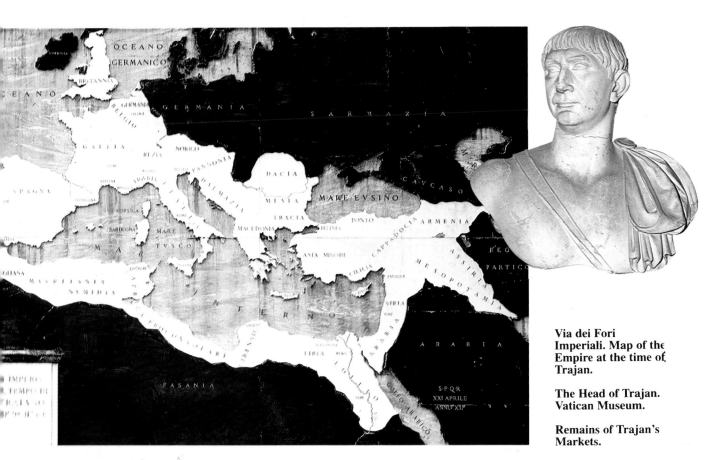

Via dei Fori
Imperiali. Map of the
Empire at the time of
Trajan.

The Head of Trajan.
Vatican Museum.

Remains of Trajan's
Markets.

poor district. On July 18th, 64 A.D. the fire started and Rome burned for six days, leaving thousands homeless. We are not sure that Nero had anything to do with it, but, in any case, he profited from the circumstance, and had his fabulous **Golden House** built.

Capitoline Museum. Portrait of Nero.

The Naumachia. Nero used to watch naval battles on the lake; later the Colosseum was built on the site, and Romans could watch the same spectacle in the Colosseum itself. Augustus had a Naumachia(lake) constructed near the Garden of Caesar by the year 2 A.D.; later Trajan built another not far from the Vatican. The XVII century Veronese engraver Onofrio Panvinio has left us this fine reconstruction of a Naumachia.

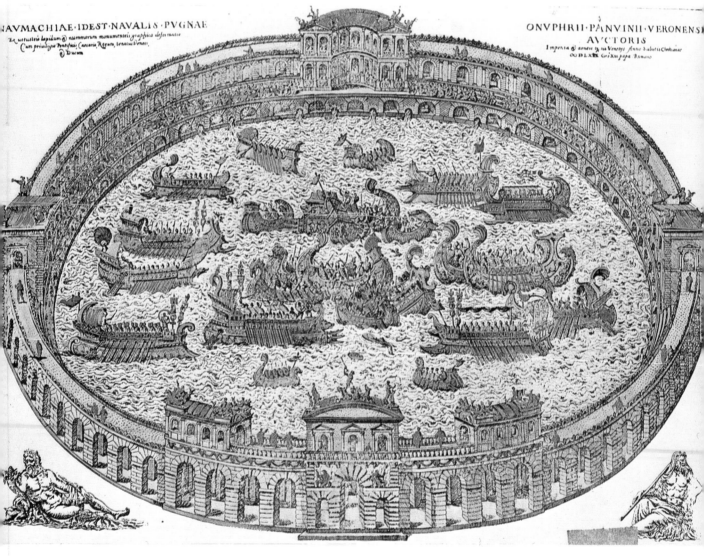

The Arch of Constantine.

The "Colossus", the gigantic statue of Nero, from which the Colosseum takes its name. A drawing by G.Gatteschi.

The building, alone, covered a square mile in the heart of Rome. Besides the imperial residence there were parks, gardens and baths, supplied by sulphur springs, which were 12 miles away and also supplied by water from the Mediterranean. There was a temple to Fortuna, built of translucent stone and a big, artificial lake for naval battles, to amuse the Emperor. A colossal gilded bronze statue of Nero, one hundred and twenty feet high, stood near the lake. In 68 A.D. Nero was in Greece, showing his abilities as an actor, when the legions in Spain revolted and proclaimed their commander, Galba, Emperor. He accepted and marched towards Rome, where the Senate decreed Nero's death. When Nero came back to Rome he found no friends and he ordered his slave to kill him, on June 9th 68 A.D. His house was partly demolished, the gilded bronze colossus was decapitated, and Apollo's head replaced that of Nero and over the site of the artificial lake the Colosseum was built; it took its name from the gigantic statue

ASTIVVS

RODAN

Mosaic dating from the 3rd century A.D., depicting combats of gladiators, kept in the Borghese Museum.

For the defeated gladiator, the sentence was often "thumb down".

The ritual salute of the gladiators to the emperor, before combat.

The lovely bronze statue of the "retiario" (gladiator armed with net and trident), reproduced by the kind permission of the Hotel Baglioni Regina in Rome. Dated 1908, it is the work of sculptor Pio Welonski.

The Colosseum

The majestic Flavian Amphitheatre, from the name of the emperors of the Flavius family who built it, known universally as the Colosseum, stands in a hollow that in Nero's time was occupied by an artificial lake in the gardens of the Domus Aurea. The construction was begun under Vespasian in around 72-75 A.D., and the building was inaugurated by Titus in the year 80. According to tradition, 40,000 slaves were employed; they were part of the 100,000 prisoners Titus had brought to Rome in the tear 70 A.d., after the destruction of Jerusalem.

The Colosseum, which could contain at least 50,000 spectators, was mainly intended for gladiator shows and wild beasts hunts and often, actual stage settings were provided to make the cruel scenes more life-like and exciting for the multitudes of spectators thirsting for blood and pleasure.

Among the shows, worthy of mention are the inaugural ones, which lasted 100 days during which 50,000 beasts and hundreds of gladiators were killed. Under Trajan, 11,000 beasts were killed and 10,000 gladiators fought there. Under Probus, in a single hunt, the roaring of one hundred young lions all released at once into the arena caused the whole amphitheatre to tremble. But the most popular were the gladiators. It is difficult to imagine the fanaticism, especially of the women, for these handsome, cruel fighters who, after a number of victories were given their freedom.

For the gladiator combats the arena was spread with sand (Latin *arena* = sand). Underneath the floor were the cells for the prisoners and the enclosures for the beasts. The large amphitheatre was mainly used during the spring and the summer, and the spectators were suitably protected from the sun by a canvas roof open in the centre, the *"velarium"*. The Colosseum was used for shows until 608 A.D. In the Middle Ages it was transformed into a fortress and in the following ages it was partly torn down to obtain building material for churches, bridges, etc. The plundering continued for centuries and was finally stopped in XIX century, when the Popes began the restoration of the remaining parts, as can be seen in the rebricked sections. The majestic monument is an example of skilful engineering. Like all Roman architecture, it is based on the principle of the arch and vault. A system of suitably distributed arches, vaults, and elliptical rings gave the structure an extremely high level of stability and safety

The Colosseum.

AVE CAESAR MORITURI TE SALUTANT!
(Hail, Caesar; those who are about to die salute you!)

On pages 105-106
Reconstruction of the Colosseum. Drawing by architect Eva Maria Varsanyi.
The exterior part of the Colosseum consists of three orders of arcades; the fourth floor has solid walls. The over 200 poles on the top supported the "velarium", the huge canvas roof which protected the spectators from the sun. Through the eighty gates, of which 76 were numbered, the spectators reached the seats assigned to them according to their social rank, in one of the four sectors into which the tiers were divided, as we see in the reconstruction. Starting from the bottom: the seven steps of the "podium", reserved for the authorities, senators, and vestals, next to the imperial box. The second row, the "low cavea", was reserved for the knights or upper class. The third sector, the "middle cavea", was for the middle class, and the top was the "maenianum summum", the section for the populace.

On pages 107-108
Reconstruction of the interior of the Colosseum, with wild beast hunt and gladiator combats. During the warm season, the "velarium", open in the centre, was spread out over the spectators. Around one hundred sailors of the fleet of Miseno, near Naples, attended to the raising and spreading out of the velarium. This operation took at least four days.
Drawing by architect Eva Maria Varsanyi.

109

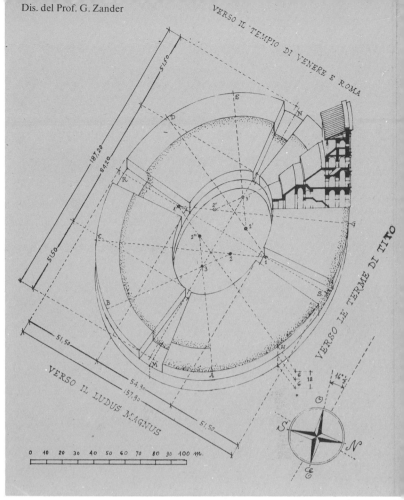

Dis. del Prof. G. Zander

VERSO IL TEMPIO DI VENERE E ROMA

VERSO LE TERME DI TITO

VERSO IL LUDUS MAGNUS

◄ **The Colosseum. Interior , as it is today.**

Recent studies have ascertained that the Colosseum was built on a huge elliptical ring foundation twelve metres thick and fifty metres wide, with a maximum diameter of one hundred and eighty-eight metres, made of concrete and blocks of granite. On this rest the load-bearing pillars of travertine. The enormous underground structure rests in turn on the clay bed of Nero's lake - that is to say on mud which enables it to absorb earth tremors and shifts in the distribution of weight. Even by today's standards it is a magnificent engineering achievement, which explains how the Colosseum has lasted for 2000 years.

The Circus Maximus

The Circus Maximus, reconstruction. Detail from the model of imperial Rome in the Museum of Roman Civilization in E.U.R. by I.Gismondi.

A Roman Chariot. Vatican Museums.

The Circus Maximus today. ▶

Christians at the Circus. XIX century engraving. ▶

Leaving the Colosseum we take Via San Gregorio Magno, between the Palatine and the Caelian hill. On the right are some remains of the acqueduct built by Claudius, and on the left is the **church of St. Gregory the Great**. This site holds the memory of the great Pope, who sent to Britain the band of Benedictines, with Saint Augustine at their head, to evangelize the country. He was also a musician and wrote the Gregorian Chants, and he was the one who had the vision of Archangel Michael over Hadrian's tomb.

At the end of Via San Gregorio, you can locate **the Circus Maximus**, in the open space on the right, the valley lying between the Palatine and the Aventine. The remains of the Imperial Palaces, where the aristocracy lived, are on the Palatine (the plebeians lived on the Aventine). The Circus Maximus was the largest stadium for chariot races. It could accommodate over 250,000 spectators. During the persecutions the majority of Christian martyrs were offered there. Now you can only see the site of the arena which was separated into two tracks by a long, low wall, the Spina.

San Paolo fuori le Mura
(St. Paul's without the Walls)

We are directed to St Paul's outside the Walls passing the modern F.A.O. building on our left, (Food and Agriculture Organization of the United Nations) and then we pass St. Paul's gate, which is another gate of the Aurelian Wall. By the gate is the Pyramid of Caius Caestius Epulone, a Roman tomb built in the style of the Egyptian pyramid, in 11 B.C. Almost three hundred years later the pyramid was included in the defensive wall built by Aurelianus. Behind the wall and the pyramid lies the **Protestant cemetery** of Rome where the two English poets, Shelley and Keats, are buried. Then we continue on the old Ostiense Way, the road leading to Ostia, the ancient seaport of Rome. It was the commercial and military harbour of Imperial Rome, at that time Ostia had a population of one hundred-thousand people. Ancient Ostia is the best preserved Roman city, after Pompei, and modern Ostia is the beach of the Romans.

Emperor Constantine built the Basilica of St.

Paul's without the Walls, over the grave of this Saint as a memorial church, as he did over the grave of St. Peter. St. Paul was beheaded at a place called "ad Aquas Salvias", known as le Tre Fontane (the Three Fountains). These three fountains welled up where St. Paul's head had touched the ground and where three churches, tended by the Trappist monks, now stand. After the martyrdom, the Saint was buried near the Ostia road and the church which Constantine built in the IV century was rebuilt more magnificently in 386 and was almost totally destroyed by fire in a few hours on July 15th, 1823, during restoration works of the wooden ceiling. The present basilica was rebuilt as a perfect reproduction of the old one with contributions from different countries. The front of the church is not facing the rising sun, and this is the only one of the patriarchal churches which does not. The present church has a quadriportico which the old one did not have, in the middle of which stands the modern statue of Saint Paul, by Obici. St. Paul is holding a sword in his hand, which is the symbol of the fight he fought for Christianity. You will recall the second letter to Timothy, his last farewell to the Christians: "For I am ready to be offe-

The Basilica of St.Paul's without the Wall. Main façade. ▶

Interior of the Basilica of St.Paul; lithograph by Benoist, XIX century. ▶

The Pyramide of Caius Sextius and Porta S.Paolo.

St.Paul's Without the Walls. The Christ Pantocrator, detail of the XIII century mosaic in tha absis.

St.Paul's without the Walls. The XIII century Cosmatesque cloister.

red, my course is finished, I fought a good fight; I have kept the faith...". The front of the church is decorated with a resplendent mosaic work by the artists of the mosaic studio of the Vatican. The door at the extreme right is the Porta Santa (the Holy Door).

Entering this church you would almost believe it to be the interior of an Imperial Roman basilica, miraculously survived from the past and perfectly preserved through the centuries; it really gives an exact idea of the basilicas of Imperial Rome. Over the main altar and the Apostle's grave, at which only the Pope celebrates Mass, is the beautiful 13th century altar canopy, by Arnolfo di Cambio, which was rescued from the fire by the triumphal arch over it. This arch had been donated to the church by Galla Placidia, queen of the Goths in the fifth century. The arch, the canopy and the apse, with the 13th century mosaic, are the only remaining parts of the old church. You will also notice the roundels, with the mosaic portraits of all the 264 Popes, including the present one. All the alabaster of the windows was donated by the Viceroy of Egypt, Mohamed Ali, and Czar Nicholas I of Russia contributed the malachite altars at the end

walls of the transept.

From the church we pass into the lovely cloister garden in the adjoining monastery. The Benedictine monastery was rebuilt, but the 13th century colonnade in its rich Cosmatesque style is original. All around are the remains of the church which burned and tombstones from the Catacombs and other graves.

San Paolo Fuori le Mura. The splendid coupled columns of the Cosmatesque cloister, some inlaid with mosaics.

fourth tour

Santa Maria Maggior (St. Mary Major) - Saint Peter In Chains - the Holy Stairs - St. John Lateran - the Catacombs - Janiculum - Trastevere

The Basilica of St.Mary ▶
Major. Main façade.

Santa Maria Maggiore is one of the four main patriarchal and pilgrimage basilicas with the Porta Santa. It stands on the Esquiline, another of the historical seven hills of Rome, and this is the first church in the West to have been dedicated to the Madonna. It was built first in 352, after the miracle of the snow. In 352 a patrician, named John, and his wife, who both wanted a child, saw the Madonna in a dream. The Madonna told them that their desire was answered and that they should build a church on the site where they would, the next morning, find snow. When they told Pope Liberius of their dream he said that he had dreamed the same dream. In the morning of the 5th of August the area of the Esquiline Hill was covered with snow (it is very hot in Rome in August).

The present church is the one built under Pope Sixtus III (432-440) to celebrate the Council of Ephesus (431), which proclaimed the Holy Motherhood of the Virgin Mary. In the front square of the Church stands a column taken from the Basilica of Maxentius in the Forum; it was dedicated to the Madonna in the XVII century. The facade was renovated by F. Fuga in 1743, in late Baroque style. In the portico, on the left, is the Porta Santa.

It is the interior of the church which is really most interesting. Of the original building, we still see the 36 columns of Greek marble taken from the temple of Juno, on the Aventine; and above the columns is a series of mosaics from the fifth century, 36 pictures representing events from the Old Testament. They are extremely well preserved, showing a strong classical inspiration and were certainly copied from old miniatures, from old illuminated stories of The Bible. They form, with the ones on the triumphal arch and the decoration of the apse the real glory of Santa Maria Maggiore. The Cosmatesque floor, the finest in that style in our chur-

ches, was added in the thirteenth century and the magnificent wooden ceiling, was built by Antonio da Sangallo, an eminent Renaissance architect, at the end of the 15th century. The ceiling was gilded with the first gold Columbus brought from America to Europe. That gold was donated by King Ferdinand of Aragon, of Spain, to the Borgia Pope Alexander VI. Over the main altar is the canopy, probably inspired by Bernini's Baldacchino in St. Peter's, designed by Fuga, the same architect responsible for the 18th century facade. In the lowered part, in front of the papal altar, and in front of the crypt, where are kept the relics of the Holy Cradle, is the kneeling statue of Pope Pius IX, the Pope who declared the dogma of the Immaculate Conception of the Virgin Mary in 1854.

Above the altar the arches decorated with fifth century mosaics, which complete the series of the ones in the central nave and depict events from the life of Mary and the childhood of Christ, still referring to the Council of Ephesus: they show less classical influence. The story begins at the top, on the left, with the Annunciation, where the Virgin Mary is unusually represented seated and spinning. The mosaics on the apse are by Torriti, 13th century, strongly influenced by Byzantine art; but the figures are loosing the absolute flatness of Byzantine style, there is a touch of life in the colorful groups of the angels. The Triumph of Mary and the Coronation are the climax of the other mosaics in this church.

The two large chapels on either side of the High Altar form the transept of the church. The one on the left was built by Pope Paul V Borghese. **The Borghese**

Chapel is known as the richest private chapel in the churches of Rome. At the main altar is a 13th century icon of the Madonna, held by a glory of angels. The frame is encrusted with precious and semiprecious stones and there is a large display of most valuable marbles all around. Above the altar is the relief with the miracle of the snow. This chapel was decorated in the seventeenth century Baroque style, but without the ostentation of the extreme Baroque. The paintings are by Cavalier d'Arpino and Guido Reni; notice the St. Francis under the arch to the left. In the crypt of the chapel are buried several members of the Borghese family, among whom is Paoline Bonaparte. Opposite is the **chapel of the Holy Sacrament**, built by Domenico Fontana under Pope Sixtus V, in 1585; its gilded-bronze ciborium is by

L. Scalzo, and it stands over the remains of the 13th century chapel, where the relics of Jesus's Crib were originally kept.

Before leaving the Church we stop for a look at the tomb of Bernini; the founder of the most adorned and elaborate artistic style was given a most humble grave, just a simple marble slab with his name on it. He received the honour of resting in this important basilica, where you find the best examples of the main styles of the last fifteen hundred years. Here, without much effort and with the knowledge of a few essential elements of styles, you can enjoy reading the history of art of fifteen centuries. In this classic basilica you find first class examples of mediaeval art as the mosaics and the cosmatesque floor: for Renaissance the ceiling by

◀ **Interior of St.Mary Major.**

◀ **St.Mary Major. The Baptistry.**

St.Mary Major: the apse with the XIII cent. mosaic decoration and the Main Altar with the canopy by F.Fuga, XVIII cent.

San Pietro in Vincoli
(St. Peter in Chains)

Interior of the Church of San Pietro in Vincoli.

The statue of Moses by Michaelangelo, detail.

San Pietro in Vincoli. Michaelangelo's Moses.

San Pietro in Vincoli. The Chains of St.Peter.

Sangallo and for the Baroque style the adornment of the Borghese chapel.

S. Pietro In Vincoli (St. Peter in Chains) This church was built about 440 A.D. by Eudoxia, the wife of Emperor Valentinian III, to be a shrine for the chains of St. Peter, which she had received from Pope Leo I (The Great). This occurred after the chains, one from the Mamertine Prison, near the Forum, and the other from the prison of Jerusalem, where St. Peter was held, according to tradition, were wrought together by miracle. The interior of the church is in the style of a Roman basilica, with 24 beautiful marble columns in Doric style; the ceiling was painted by Parodi, XVII century and the floor has been recently restored. The most important feature of St. Peter in Chains is, in any case, the statue of **Moses by Michelangelo**. He made this statue for Pope Julius II, nephew of Sixtus IV. Sixtus IV, before being elected pope, had been titular cardinal of St. Peter in Chains and this title he gave later to his nephew, Julian della Rovere. Julian became pope, with the name of Julius II; he is the pope who started rebuilding St. Peter's at the Vatican, who had the ceiling of the Sistine Chapel painted by Michelangelo and had the Stanze painted by Raphael. Well, as soon as Julius II was elected, he started thinking of his magnificent mausoleum to be placed in the new St. Peter's church and he summoned to Rome Michelangelo, who had just astonished his townsmen with the colossal statue of David. Michelangelo planned for the pope a huge monument, three-storied, four-sided, decorated with 44 statues of the size of Moses and 28 reliefs. The contract was stipulated, Michelangelo was soon off to Carrara to choose marbles for his gigantic undertaking. He spent seven months there. When Michelangelo came back to Rome, the Pope had changed his mind, as he had been persuaded by Michelangelo's competitors against the project. He tried, unsuccessfully, to settle with the pope and after a quarrel he left Rome. Later they were reconciled, but he was given other works, and the monument was

never finished. The 44 colossal statues dwindled to one and Julius II never saw his mausoleum finished.

At length, after innumerable vicissitudes and controversies, in 1545 when Michelangelo was 70, and 40 years after he had made his first plan for the mausoleum of Julius II, he completed the monument we see now in St. Peter in Chains and was finally released from that contract by the relatives of the dead pope. The statue of Moses was probably finished one or two years after he had painted the ceiling of the Sistine Chapel.

The figure of the prophet is very similar to the figuers he painted on the ceiling of the Sistine Chapel. Moses has the same majesty and power and is one of the many magnified human figures created by Michelangelo, reflecting his concepts of Man and his philosophy. The statue of Moses, more than any other by Michelangelo, embodies his sentiments and thoughts; it portrays exactly the fervent emotions, the anger, the conception, the disappointment and the sorrow of Moses in a dramatic moment; come down from Mt. Sinai after receiving the Ten Commandments from God. He found his people worshipping the Golden Calf. Michelangelo has represented in the marble, with perfect exactness, the psychology of that moment; Moses holds the tablets under his right arm tightly, as if to defend from heresy the Code of Law on which the human rights of generations to come would be based.

La Scala Santa
(The Holy Stairs)

Church of the Scala Santa: The "Acherotipa" painting (i.e."not painted by human hand") of the Saviour, in the Chapel of San Lorenzo. In the Midlle Ages it was belived that this picture had been painted by the angels

St. John Lateran. Statue of the Emperor Constantine.

The Holy Stairs.

San Giovanni in Laterano (St. John Lateran)

The façade of St. John Lateran seen from the lovely modern monument to St. Francis of Assisi.

Aereal view of St. John Lateran and the Palazzo Lateranense.

Approaching **St. John Lateran** you notice the Egyptian obelisk which Constantius II brought to Rome in the 4th century, and put in the Circus Maximus as a companion to the one brought by Augustus, nearly four hundred years before and which now stands in Piazza del Popolo. It was re-erected here in 1585 and is the biggest and the oldest one of the fourteen obelisks of Rome. It dates from the fifteenth century B.C. and stood originally before the Temple of Ammon in Thebes and it stands in front of the **Lateran Palace**, built in XVI century. This palace where the Lateran Treaty was signed, used to house the Lateran Collection, which has recently been moved to the Vatican. It is now the Vicariate. Domenico Fontana, XVI century, is responsible for the architecture. Nearby is the beautiful octagonal Baptistry, built in the V century, and recently restored.

The Laterani, leading noble people of imperial Rome, were the owners of this area, which became property of Constantine as a dowry of his wife, Fausta. After his victory, Constantine gave this area and the palace of Plautius Lateranus to Pope Melchiades in 325 A.D. and so the territorial acquisition of the Church began. The Cathedral of Rome was founded there and for about a thousand years was the seat of the Bishop of Rome. The only remaining part of the old papal palace is on top of the Holy Stairs **Scala Santa**, the **Sancta Sanctorum**, - the Pope's private chapel. The church of the Holy Stairs was originally built in the fourth century to enshrine the staircase built with the 28 marble steps, believed the ones from Pilate's palace in Jerusalem and brought to Rome by St. Helena. Jesus ascended these stairs several times when he underwent sentencing and flagellation; the faithful use to climb them on their knees. The present church was rebuilt in 1585 by Sixtus V. After getting an impression of the religious significance of the Scala Santa, we walk over to the Cathedral. From far away you have probably watched the giant statues (twenty feet high) at the top of the facade and silhouetted against the Roman sky. They represent Christ, in the Center, and the Doctors of the Church, St. Vincent. St. Ambrose, St. Augustine etc.

The facade of St. John was built by Alexander Galilei in 1735. In the portico, to the right, is the Porta Santa. The central bronze door, dating from 305 A.D., was removed from the Curia(Roman Senate) in the Forum, in 1650. At the far inside end of the portico on the left is a restored statue of Emperor Constantine, one of the few statues we have of him. Not even the Romans saw much of Constantine; he was born near the Danube, was educated in Asia and he visited Rome only three times in his life. The church was rebuilt several times and the last reconstruction dates back to 1650, by the Baroque architect **Borromini.** Inside the central nave you find the imposing statues of the Apostles, in the recesses against the piers. The statues are by the followers of Bernini. Above the piers are the reliefs by Algardi, depicting analogies of the Old and New Testament. From the previous·reconstructions is the Cosmatesque floor dating from XIV century. The ceiling is by **Daniel da Volterra**, a disciple of Michelangelo, XVI century. The canopy of the High Altar has a touch of Gothic style and dates from the XV century. The most precious relics of

St.John Lateran: interior

St.John Lateran: the apse and the Cathedra (the Papal Throne). ▶

St. John Lateran. Fragment of Giotto's fresco with Pope Boniface VIII solemnly announcing, from the loggia of the Cathedral, the opening of the Church's first Holy Year in 1300. ▶

St.John Lateran are kept under the canopy beyond the gilded grill. They are the skull bones of St. Peter and St. Paul, in the head of the statues of the saints. In the lowered part in front of the main alter is the bronze grave of Pope Martin V (Colonna). (The founder of this princely house was a crusader who brought to Rome from Jerusalem the column of the Scourging of Christ).

In the transept on the left is the altar of the **Blessed Sacrament**, above the altar are the relics of the table of Jesus's Last Supper. On the right is the monumental pipe organ, from 1598. At the end of the last century the apse was rebuilt; and there is the Throne of the Bishop of Rome.

Above the Papal Throne (Cattedra) is a reproduction, of the 13th century mosaic by Torriti, and the two new pipe organs. This church certainly cannot compete with the classic beauty and authentic antiquity of Santa Maria Maggiore, but from the historical and religious aspect, this is the most important of all Christian churches.

Its rank is "Head and Mother" of all Churches in Rome and in the world. It is the seat of the Pope. When the Pope goes out of the Vatican, for the first time after his Coronation, he goes to St. John's to take possession of it. This church certainly saw its greatest splendor during the Middle Ages, when the Lateran was still the residence of the Popes. Then the Papacy was driven out of Rome by the riots and violence, and when the Pope came back to Rome after the captivity in Avignon, the Papal Palace of the Lateran had been completely ruined by fire and was inhabitable and the Pope went to live at the Vatican.

Before leaving the church, notice the fragment of a restored fresco painting behind the first pier, on the right of the central nave, a restored fresco painting of **Pope Boniface VIII** announcing the beginning of the first Holy Year in the history of the Church in 1300. This fresco was painted by Giotto, who came to Rome as a pilgrim for the Jubilee Year

The bust of Emperor Caracalla. Capitoline Museum.

The ruins of the Baths of Caracalla.

The Baths of Caracalla and the Ancient Appian Way

To reach the ancient Appian Way and the Catacombs we will pass the imposing remains of the **Baths of Caracalla**. These were the second largest public baths of Imperial Rome built by Emperor Caracalla in 206 A.D.; the biggest were built one hundred years later by Emperor Diocletian. In Rome there were eleven big *Thermae*.

The Thermae (baths) were a kind of huge club houses, used mainly for bathing, where the Romans used to entertain. Caracalla's Baths were the most richly decorated; many works of art were recovered there. Sculptures and mosaics, which can be seen in the museums of Rome and Naples. Driving by, you can send a reverent salute to the English poet Shelley, who in the Spring of 1819 wrote most of his "Prometeus Unbound" *"upon the mountainous ruins of the Baths of Caracalla"*.

As soon as you pass these ruins you take the **ancient Appian Way**, the first military road built by the Romans. It was first built to connect Rome with the southern part of Italy, especially with Capua, north of Naples, which was the second most important Italian city in the 4th century B.C. It was then completed as far as Brindisi (Brundisium) on the Adriatic coast and also became the shortest route to the Near East. Brindisi was the sea-port from which the Romans sailed to Greece, Turkey, etc. The road was started in 312 B.C. by Consul Appius Claudius. These were the first miles of the huge network of highways the Romans left over the Empire, in total some 60 thousand miles of road,. (After the fall of Rome no new roads were built in Europe for about 15 centuries), 85

Roman bridges are still in use. During the days of the Empire, the first ten miles of the Appian Way were flanked by the monumental graves of patrician Roman families. These ten miles of monuments certainly formed quite an approach to the capital of the Empire. The Romans were not allowed to bury their dead in the city; they built their tombs along the roads and most of them were on the Via Appia, the *Regina Viarum* (the Queen of the Roads). After we have passed the **tomb of the Scipio family** (the family of warriors, Scipio the Aemilianus, Scipio the Africanus, etc.) we meet the **arch of Drusus**, another warrior, better known as Germanicus because of his victories on the Rhine. He was the younger brother of Tiberius, married to Mark Antony's daughter Antonia, and was the father of Claudius, whom Agrippina poisoned to get the throne for her son Nero. Next comes the turreted **gate of St. Sebastian**, the largest and best preserved of the gates in the Aurelian Wall.

Down further on the left is the small famous Chapel of **Domine Quo Vadis**, built over the site where, according to tradition, St. Peter, fleeing from death during Nero's persecution, had the vision of Christ and uttered the famous three words "Domine Quo Vadis?" (Lord, where goes Thou?) and the Lord replied that he was on his way to Rome to be crucified again because Peter had abandoned the Christians in danger. Peter went back to Rome and was crucified. The chapel was rebuilt in the XVII century by the Barberini family. Two more minutes drive and you are at the Catacombs.

The Catacombs

There are about forty-five Catacombs around Rome, and the most frequently visited are those along the Appian Way; St. Calixtus, St. Sebastian and the Domitilla Catacombs. They are tended by different religious orders and the areas are under the jurisdiction of the Vatican State. There are Pagan, Jewish and, of course, the Christian Catacombs. The term Catacomb was originally applied only to those of St. Sebastian. The others were merely called cemeteries (form Greek koimeterion - a sleeping chamber or burial place).

The majority of the Catacombs are Christian because Christians liked to be buried in the same way as Christ: in a cave, wrapped in linen, and also because most of them belonged to the poor classes and could not afford rich mausoleums. The underground galleries were dug because the surface area could not be exceeded, so they dug more deeply underneath. This explains the five or six levels of the Catacombs. The total estimated length of the galleries is about 500 miles, and about six million people were buried in a span of three hundred years.

The catacombs were not a secret place and were known to everyone, but the Roman law was very clear and compassionate about graves. Burial places were considered sacred and nobody could touch or violate them, that is the reason why persecuted Christians would occasionally escape to those underground labyrinths.

Some tours will go to the Catacombs of St. Calixtus, others to those of Domitilla or St. Sebastian.

The Catacombs of St. Calixtus is one of the largest, and in the third century it became the official cemetery of the Christian Church; several Popes were buried there. The inscriptions on their graves are very simple, and most of them are written in Greek, which was the first official language of the Church. Saint Cecilia is buried in this Catacomb. She is the patron saint of musicians. According to tradition, she heard such heavenly sounds that to express them she invented the organ. The Saint was martyred with the heat of the steam bath in her patrician house in Trastevere, where the Church of St. Cecilia now stands. After many hours without being harmed, she was finally beheaded, but her head could not be severed. In 1599 her coffin was opened and her body was found intact. The sculptor Stefano Maderno made the statue of the Saint exactly as he saw her. This is the replica you see in the crypt - the original is in the Church of St. Cecilia at Trastevere.

The Catacombs of St. Sebastian. In this Catacomb on the Appian Way, during the persecution of Emperor Valerian, the relics of St. Peter and St. Paul were moved for safe-keeping, so that the place became an object of cult and pilgrimage, confirmed by the "graffiti" written on the walls by the pilgrims; "Peter and Paul pray for us", "Peter and Paul remember us", etc. St. Sebastian is one of the saints of whom you are more frequently reminded, all through Europe, as all art collections have one or more pictures of the martyr, his beautiful young body stuck with arrows. He was a Gaul of Narbonne, an officer in Diocletian's army. The church of St. Sebastian was built over his grave, and there is also the original marble from the site of the *Domine Quo Vadis*, with the foot-print of Christ.

The Domitilla Catacombs.

In this large Catacomb, are fine paintings. You enter it from the basilica(built at the end of the IV century) of the Saints Nereus and Achilleus. The area of this Catacomb is called that of Ampliatus. In 1881 a tomb was discovered with the name "Ampliati" engraved in Roman lettering; he is possibly the same Ampliatus mentioned by St. Paul in his "Epistle to the Romans" - "Salute Ampliatus my beloved in The Lord"...   .

In each of the Catacombs the fathers provide excellent guides. You will certainly feel the atmosphere of utter faith and complete trust of the early Christians as witnessed by the innumerable inscriptions and paintings, all expressing Christian brotherhood and charity. Continuing further along the ancient Appian Way you pass the remains of the **Circus of Maxentius**, the Emperor defeated by Constantine. He built a stadium for chariot races in the fourth century, A.D., near the mausoleum he built for his son, Romulus, who died at the age of nine. Then the most imposing of the graves which lined the historical road, the **tomb of**

Catacombs of St.Domitila, the Good Shepherd. Fresco painting of III cent. A.D.

Via Appia Antica. The tomb of Cecilia Metella. ▶

Catacombs of St. Domitilla: the underground basilica of St. Nereus and St. Achilleus, of the IV century A. D.

Via Appia Antica. Still today, this historic road offers sights ▶
which inspired many artists of the past.

Cecilia Metella, daughter of the Roman General Quintus Metellus, called Creticus for he had conquered the Island of Crete. Cecilia was married to one of the sons of Crassus, the wealthy Roman who paid Julius Caesar's debts and shared the triumph with him. The grave, built in the first century B.C. and so familiar a landmark of the Roman Campagna, was given by Pope Boniface VIII Caetani to his relatives, who made it into a donjon, They also had the bright idea of building a bridge across the road to exact a toll from travellers to and from Rome. A bit further along the road, parts of original paving, with large cobble-stones are visible.

The historical picturesque promenade will remind you of the many descriptions of the Appian Way by Horace Walpole, Nathaniel Hawthorne, Robert Browning and Lord Byron. Music lovers will recall the Pines of Rome by Respighi, the last part of the melody being inspired by the trees of the Appian Way.

Janiculum and Trastevere

No visit to Rome would be complete without taking in the panoramic view of the city from high up on the Janiculum Hill, the hill which the Romans dedicated to Janus, the God with two faces. In the large open space on the highest point of the hill there stands the equestrian statue of Giuseppe Garibaldi by Gallori, and this stands at the centre of the busts of his soldiers, the "Garibaldini", which are scattered all around the park, as a memorial to the defence of the Roman Republic during the Risorgimento, Italy's nineteenth century national resurgence.

From this piazza we can see the domes and roofs of Trastevere, the old quarter which spreads out at the foot of the hill. Trastevere (from Trans-Tiberin, the other side of the Tiber) was the centre of Rome's oriental community in classical times - and especially of the Jews. It has been inhabited without a break for more than two thousand years, and is considered to be the most "Roman" of all the districts of Rome. Its inhabitants, known as the "Trasteverini" boast that they are the only authentic descendants of the true Roman stock. In the huddle of old houses, in the mediaeval churches and monasteries and in the buildings of the Renaissance, we can see the evidence of Trastevere's thousands of years of history, but the spirit of the Trasteverini themselves is felt most of all in the typical local haunts where one can still hear the characteristic slang used by Belli and Trilussa, and the natives of the area still keep up the traditional ways and folklore of the area, despite the sophistication which has crept in recent years because of the many colonies of foreigners who now live there.

Among the churches of Trastevere we should mention Santa Maria in Trastevere in particular. It stands on one side of the square named after it, and it is outstanding for its mediaeval structure and for the mosaics and the wealth of other treasures which it possesses.

The Acqua Paola Fountain on the Janiculum, XVII cent. built by Pope Paul V, Borghese.

Santa Maria in Trastevere. The splendid ceiling with the painting of the Assumption by Domenichino, XVII cent.

Church of Santa Maria in Trastevere.

fifth tour
Tivoli - Hadrian's Villa and Villa d'Este

After the four tours dedicated to the exploration of churches, museums and ruins, it will be relaxing to drive out to the Roman Campagna, away from the strident roar of the city.

Leaving for Tivoli we'll pass the modern railway station, **Stazione Termini**, noting the remains of the old city wall, known as **the Servian Wall**, the oldest defence wall of Rome, built in the IV century B.C.; **the University City**, completed in 1953 (about 100,000 students), and the mediaeval church of **S. Lorenzo Fuori le Mura**, another Basilica ad Corpus (Basilica at the Body) founded by Constantine over the grave of St. Lawrence. It was renovated in the XIII century and was bombed in 1943,

and afterwards restored.

We are now on the **Tiburtina** Way, one of the Roman Highways which takes its name from Tibur (the ancient Tivoli). This road continues across the Appennines over to Pescara on the Adriatic coast. After we pass the sulphur-water springs, the Acque Albule, and the quarries of travertine stone, the same quarries which supplied the travertine blocks to build the Colosseum, we'll see the old, restored Roman bridge, **Ponte Lucano**. Near this bridge over the Aniene, the tributary of the Tiber which feeds the fountains of Villa d'Este, stands the imposing Tomb of the Plautii family from the I century, B.C. Then we enter **Villa Adriana**.

Hadrian's Villa

This imperial residence was started in the year 125 A.D. and was finished in 135 A.D., though other buildings were added later. Emperor Hadrian, one of the greatest personalities of the Roman world, a great soldier, a statesman, an architect and a poet, was also a great traveller, one of the few Emperors who visited every province of his immense Empire which he inherited from his adoptive father, Trajan, in 117 A.D. However Greece was his great love, which also dominated his architectural ideas, as you may recall from your visit to the Pantheon and as it is evident in the remaining parts of the villa we are going to visit.

The model of the Villa Adriana, recently made, and which we'll see first, will help us to visualize its original appearence. There we see the reproduction of the 25 buildings which formed the residence and in which, according to tradition, the Emperor wished to reproduce outstanding monuments from the various parts of the Empire. Although there is not evidence of these buildings being replicas of others, some resemblance can be found in some of them. The huge wall, standing

nearby, sustained the roof of the long covered walk of the perystile with a central pool, named **Poecile**, from the famous portico of Athens which was decorated with paintings by the most prominent Greek artists. As soon as we find ourselves beyond the long honeycombed tufa wall, we realize the enchantment of Villa Adriana, we are in a real "classical landscape with ruins", one of the places which inspired the English-landscaped parks, and which also gave inspiration to the painters of half Europe. This is perhaps the reason why Hadrian's Villa holds an immediate, magic appeal for the visitor. Throughout the ruins the predominant characteristic will be its interpenetration of vegetation and ruins similar to the original very close association of house and garden, as we saw in the model. For a serious study of Roman architecture there are places, such as Pompei and Ancient Ostia, where buildings are in a much better state of preservation, but much

pleasure, I believe, can be gained simply by wandering through the ruins of Villa Adriana, without any knowledge of them. The pathetic remains of these buildings, the broken columns, the fragments of antique reliefs and mosaics, or marble floors, lying half concealed by the colored carpet of field flowers, will console the layman for the difficulty of identifying the component parts of Hadrian's varying architectural lines. We'll continue as far as **the Canopo** inspired by a place of that name near Alexandria in Egypt (a valley with a canal lined with porticoes and shops), and decorated with Greek cariatides.

The only part of Hadrian's Villa to retain any evidence of its past splendor is the **Teatro Marittimo** (the Maritime Theater), built in the form of a circular portico, enriched by the Ionic columns and showing most perfect proportions. It lies between the Libraries and the Hall of the Greek Philosophers. Emperor Hadrian had filled

◀ **Portrait of Emperor Hadrian.**

◀ **Model of Hadrian's Villa by I.Gismondi.**

Hadrian's Villa: the Canopus.

this place with innumerable works of art, and already in the late period of the Empire, the plundering started and continued for centuries; a real gold-mine for archaelogists. All museums of note in the world have something from Hadrian's Villa. The Emperor did not live long enough to enjoy the place created by his genius and originality. In the last months of his life, he went to die at Baiae, (138 A.D.) on the sunny Bay of Naples, where he composed his address to his Soul, the famous five lines later to be written on his grave:

Hadrian's Villa: a Capital

Animula, vagula, blandula,
Hospes comesque corporis,
Quae nunc abibis in loca,
Pallidula, rigida, nudula,
Nec ut soles dabis jocos?

Soul of mine, pretty one, fitting one,
Guest and partner of my clay,
Whither wilt thou hie away,
Pallid one, rigid one, naked one
Never to play again, never to play?

By Charles Merivale we have a very accurate translation:

Hadrian's Villa: the Maritime Theatre.

Villa d'Este

After Villa Adriana we reach Tivoli, through the rather steeply rising road flanked by the very old olive trees. Tivoli, the ancient Tibur, was already occupied by the Romans in the IV century B.C. It is located on the Tiburtine hills, the foothills of the Appennines, the range of mountains crossing all Italy from the French border to the tip of the boot. Tivoli was always a resort place for the Romans; in ancient times prominent personalities and emperors, such as Sallustius, Oratius, Maecenas, Trajan and Hadrian, built their villas there.

From the square where we park we see a XV century fortress, the Rocca Pia, built by Pope Pius II. Tivoli has numerous antiquities and mediaeval structures, but its main attraction is the **Villa d'Este** with its fountains.

This villa was the creation of Cardinal Ippolito d'Este of Ferrara, son of Alfonso d'Este and Lucrezia Borgia; a shrewd diplomat who played an important role in the political and ecclesiastical events of his time, and gained the Cardinal's hat; in 1550 he received the governorship of Tivoli. The place didn't have much to offer to a man brought up in the splendor of a princely court, and with an inborne taste for art and refinement, so he started immediately to build his magnificent palace, out of an old

Benedictine cloister adjoining the mediaeval church of S. Maria Maggiore. There he would be surrounded by artists and men of culture, and following the fashion of the great Roman families of the XVI century, he had his pleasure gardens laid out on the slope of the hill, for which an entire section of the town was demolished. On the spacious terraces of his villa the Cardinal and his humanist friends would stroll, discussing the works of the classical poets.

The plan of the villa was designed by Pirro Ligorio and was carried out by G. Galvani; the fresco painting decoration was executed by G. Muziano, F. Zuccari and L. Agresti, and the sculptures, with which the gardens were adorned, were supplied by the excavations from the neighbouring Villa Adriana.

Sculptors and engineers contributed to the instalment of fountains, waterfalls and pools, and to feed them, two canals were dug to collect the water of the Aniene and of the Rivella. The fountains still work on the original hydraulic system.

The Villa remained the property of the d'Este family

Villa d'Este: the Walk of the Hundred Fountains.

Villa d'Este: the Ovata
Fountain.

until Ercole III d'Este left it to his only daughter Maria Beatrice, wife of the Archduke Ferdinand of Austria and thus the Villa passed to he Hapsburgs, and then in turn to the Hohenlohe family. In the last century extensive hospitality was given in the Villa to famous Austrian artists, Franz Liszt among them. At the beginning of World War I the Italian State confiscated it, finding it neglected and deprived of its most valuable ornaments. Restorations gave the villa its original aspect and the waterworks were repaired.

Passing through the XV century courtyard of the Benedictine monastery, we'll go down to the lower apartment, crossing the central hall, with frescoes by Muziano and Zuccari and a pretty fountain, with simulated rocks and mosaic works. Just outside this room an extensive view of the old part of Tivoli opens up and away in the distance are the towns of Sant'Angelo Romano and Palombara.

Walking down the paths lined with trees, we'll discover the magnificent fountains which have made this place unique in the world. The most spectacular of them are: the **Fountain of Rometta** (Fountain of little Rome), decorated with midget reproductions of famous ancient Roman buildings: the walk of **One Hundred Fountains**, with the long wall of the avenue turned into a fantasy of ships, obelisks, eagles and fleur-de-lis (these latter are a part of Este's coat-of-arms); from them water jets fall into the lower level; the **Fountain of the Hydraulic Organ** is the culmination of the gardens of Villa d'Este, a marvel of hydraulic engineering. This fountain could play music when water passed through the pipes of a huge organ.

On the central axis of the gardens, at midlevel, is the **Fountain of the Dragons**; the statues of the dragons we-

Villa d'Este: the Ovata Fountain at night.

re, according to tradition, put there overnight, when Pope Gregory announced to the Cardinal his intention of visiting the villa in 1572. The dragon was part of the Pope's coat-of-arms.

The Fountain of the Ovata has a most theatrical effect; in it the work of man merges with nature with the greatest harmony.

Villa d'Este: The Goddess Rome.
Detail of the Rometta Fountain.

Villa d'Este: the Fountain of the Dragons at night.

Villa d'Este: the Fountain of the Pipe Organ. ▶

Testi di Tullio Polidori
Grafica: Tullio Polidori e Beppe Fontana
Fotografie: Riccardo de Antonis - Osvaldo Ottaviani - Bruno Fiorina - Sin Ici Wakazuki
Foto Musei Vaticani - Reverenda Fabbrica di S. Pietro - AFE
Servizio Fotografico dell'Osservatore Romano - SIE
Pubbli Aer Foto - Roberto Romei - Claudio Tini - Franco Marzi
Tullio Polidori e archivio dell'editore.
Selezioni: Fotolito Gamba s.r.l.

Stampato nel mese di Gennaio 2008
da: GP srl - Tel. 06 6536336 - Roma